"Augustine of Hippo is the p
honesty became a *confessio* r
the greatest literary masterpieces. Father Turek shows us why by
reading the *Confessions* precisely as they should be read: boldly and
without the trappings of academic jargon. Anyone who spends a few
minutes each day reading Fr. Turek's reflections will understand why
Saint Augustine has become the 'best friend' of so many Christians,
including myself."

—Msgr. Daniel B. Gallagher, papal latinist

Lent with
Saint Augustine

Waldemar Turek

LITURGICAL PRESS
Collegeville, Minnesota

www.litpress.org

Cover design by Stefan Killen Design. Cover photo © Thinkstock.

Originally published as *Historia pewnego nawrócenia: Wielki Post ze św. Augustynem.* © 2012 Wydawnictwo WAM. English translation by Thomasz Koper.

1   2   3   4   5   6   7   8   9

Library of Congress Cataloging-in-Publication Data

Turek, Waldemar, 1962–
    [Historia pewnego nawrócenia. English]
    Lent with Saint Augustine / Waldemar Turek.
      pages   cm
    ISBN 978-0-8146-3760-9 — ISBN 978-0-8146-3785-2 (ebooks)
    1. Augustine, Saint, Bishop of Hippo. Confessiones.
  2. Lent—Meditations.   I. Title.
    BR65.A62T8713   2014
    270.2092—dc23   2014009826

For Priests and Students

of the Pontifical Scots College in Rome,

commending them to the intercession of St. Augustine,

with loving memory

the author

Contents

Preface

During Lent in 2010 I hosted a series of five-minute segments titled "The Story of a Conversion: Reading St. Augustine's *Confessions*" for the Polish-language broadcast of Vatican Radio. In each segment I commented on selected fragments of this literary masterpiece, a spiritual history of the bishop of Hippo, in which the author emphasizes above all the help that he has received from God on the road to true happiness. The *Confessions*, permeated with an atmosphere of devout spirituality, is a collection of prayerful deliberations on God, man, the world, time, and eternity that appeals to contemporary people and, incidentally, provides a valuable aid in experiencing the season of Lent.

I am happy that these broadcasts, expanded with the passages of the gospel read on Sundays during Lent, have been published in Polish, Italian, and now English.

I would like to extend my deepest gratitude to all those who showed me kindness and provided help in my work on this text and I pray, through the intercession of St. Augustine, that they may be blessed with the grace of understanding God in increasingly deep and profound ways.

Father Waldemar Turek

1

"Your hand is not pushed away by human obduracy"

—*Confessions* 5.1.1

❑ ❑ ❑

Lent begins. Once again in our lives, we hear the words of the psalmist, so dear to our hearts: "For I know my transgressions, and my sin is ever before me" (Ps 51:3).

It is a special time in our spiritual journey—a time of deeper contemplation of life, vocation, and suffering in light of the work of Christ over two thousand years ago. We reflect upon our failures, sins, and shortcomings, but above all on God's mercy as he reaches out to us—much like the father in the parable of the Prodigal Son.

Mercy: a word of special significance to St. Augustine, who put in writing the story of his conversion and the graces that God bestowed upon him. He compiled them in his *Confessions*, a collection of pious ponderings on matters of the divine and the human, on the world, time, and eternity. Permeated by passionate devotion, the *Confessions* still appeals strongly to contemporary readers and may provide an important aid in properly experiencing the journey of Lent.

"Accept the sacrifice of my confessions," St. Augustine prays, "offered to you by the power of this tongue of mine which you

have fashioned and aroused to confess to your name; bring healing to all my bones and let them exclaim, *Lord, who is like you?*
A person who confesses to you is not informing you about what
goes on within him, for a closed heart does not shut you out,
nor is your hand pushed away by human obduracy; you melt it
when you choose, whether by showing mercy or by enforcing
your claim, and from your fiery heat no one can hide."[1]

Man can make his heart obdurate, writes St. Augustine, but
God can break through if that is His will. There are as many
definitions of Lent as there are ways of experiencing it. Following
the thought of St. Augustine, then, we may describe it as a time
of opening our souls in order to help God in softening our hearts.

---

[1] *Confessions* 5.1.1 (113). Page numbers in parentheses refer to the
English translation by Maria Boulding, OSB (Hyde Park, NY: New City
Press, 1997).

2

"An unquiet heart"

—*Confessions* 1.1.1

❏ ❏ ❏

Who is God? Who is man? Who am I? Saint Augustine asked these questions after going through the painful experience of distancing himself from God, remaining in sin, human failures, and constant anxiety. When he started writing his *Confessions*, he was able to put most of those problems in the past, but questions about God, man, and his fate remained present.

Furthermore, he began to refine, organize, and analyze those questions. What place, he asked, do I occupy in this divinely made world? Who am I for God and for the people I encounter in my daily life? What is the nature of my true happiness?

These eternal questions are ever-present in the mind of the author, who put down the search for answers in the pages of his *Confessions*. Right there in its first paragraphs he talks about the grandeur, magnificence, might, and wisdom of God—but also the meanness, weakness, hubris, and anxiety of man.

"Great are you, O Lord, and exceedingly worthy of praise; your power is immense, and your wisdom beyond reckoning. And so we humans, who are a due part of your creation, long to praise you—we who carry our mortality about with us, carry the evidence of our sin and with it the proof that you thwart the proud. Yet these humans, due part of your creation as they are,

3

still do long to praise you. You stir us so that praising you may bring us joy, because you have made us and drawn us to yourself, and our heart is unquiet until it rests in you."[2]

Who is God to me? Who is man to me? Who am I? We fear questions like these because they seem too difficult, and so we leave them unanswered for too long. Lent provides the perfect opportunity to face them, in order to define our own spiritual state. We do not have to turn to philosophical inquiries, scientific investigations, or precise analyses. Saint Augustine states that we are a due part of God's creation and, as such, we are marked with sin and pride. He immediately adds, however, that in this element of His creation lies an immense longing to praise God, a desire that is integral to our nature. This is the way we were created and we go through life carrying some internal anxiety, which—from a spiritual standpoint—might prove useful.

Anna Popławska makes a similar confession in the pages of *Życie Duchowe* (Spiritual Life) magazine: "I was not able to pray. Or rather, I did not put enough effort in it. I fell asleep too quickly at night, weighed down by the burdens of the day, and in the morning I did not have the time. . . . I heard a constant voice of anxiety and longing, and in my heart of hearts I prayed: Lord, don't let the voice stop racking me, don't let it go away. There will come a time when I will follow it."[3]

---

[2] *Confessions* 1.1.1 (39).
[3] Anna Popławska, "Czas poszukiwania," *Życie Duchowe* 59 (2009): 104.

Friday after Ash Wednesday

3

"I praise you for my earliest days and my infancy"

—*Confessions* 1.6.10

❑ ❑ ❑

After the invocation, which is a form of very personal prayer, St. Augustine proceeds to describe and analyze his life from a spiritual standpoint, beginning at early childhood. It is a detailed retrospection of an experienced and spiritually deep man who longs to comprehend the journey along which God had led him since conception. Watching children's gestures and behavior proves helpful to his *Confessions* in this task.

"Confess to you I will, Lord of heaven and earth, and praise you for my earliest days and my infancy, which I do not remember. You allow a person to infer by observing others what his own beginnings were like. . . . Already I had existence and life, and as my unspeaking stage drew to a close I began to look for signs whereby I might communicate my ideas to others. Where could a living creature like this have come from, if not from you, Lord? Are any of us skillful enough to fashion ourselves? Could there be some channel hollowed out from some other source through which existence and life might flow to us, apart from yourself, Lord, who create us? Could we derive existence and life from anywhere other than you, in whom to be and to live are not two different realities, since supreme being and supreme life are one and the same? . . .

"What does it matter to me, if someone does not understand this? Let such a person rejoice even to ask the question, 'What does this mean?' Yes, let him rejoice in that, and choose to find by not finding rather than by finding fail to find you."[4]

Saint Augustine gives thanks to God for the gift of life and his infancy—that mysterious time to which his memories do not reach. He was not aware then of what was happening in and around him. For him that is yet another proof that he must have been shaped and given life by someone. In other words: created.

How do we perceive the earliest years of our lives, obscured by the mists of time? Stanisław Morgalla, SJ, a Jesuit priest and a professor at the Pontifical Gregorian University's Institute of Psychology, explains: "One's childhood and one's recollection of it are two different things. The former is only granted once in a lifetime and, like the river of Heraclitus's parable, it cannot be entered twice. But the memory of our childhood and, in fact, all of our past is not clear, given once, or unchanging. Quite the opposite, it grows and develops with us. . . . It is entirely up to us to choose to be 'victims' or 'authors' of it, whether to bear it passively and return to it painfully or actively face it and transform it anew."[5]

---

[4] *Confessions* 1.6.10 (44–45).
[5] Stanisław Morgalla, "Stać się dzieckiem," *Życie Duchowe* 54 (2008): 6.

4

"Rejoice over salvation of soul"

—*Confessions* 8.3.6

☐ ☐ ☐

Saint Augustine's *Confessions* are a form of honest and deep prayer, through which the author attempts to understand at least some stages of his spiritual life. By describing his personal experiences, he wants to illustrate (for the reader's benefit) the internal mechanisms that govern humans and their actions. The words he directs at God brim with references to persons, events, and passages of the Holy Bible. The Bible demonstrates how different is the thinking of God and humans, how dissimilar are the ways in which God and we attribute value. How can one, for example, explain with human logic why there is more joy in heaven from one repentant sinner than from many just persons who need no penance?

"O God, who are so good, what is it in the human heart that makes us rejoice more intensely over the salvation of a soul which is despaired of but then freed from grave danger, than we would if there had always been good prospects for it and its peril slighter? You too, merciful Father, yes, even you are more joyful over one repentant sinner than over ninety-nine righteous people who need no repentance. And we likewise listen with overflowing gladness when we hear how the shepherd carries back on exultant shoulders the sheep that had strayed, and how the coin is returned to your treasury as neighbors share the glee of the woman who found it."[6]

It is easy to see a relation between the passage above and today's reading of the Bible, which describes the calling of Matthew the tax-collector. "[Jesus] said to him 'Follow me.' And he got up, left everything, and followed him. Then Levi gave a great banquet for him in his house" (Luke 5:27-29). One might say: here is the sinner, whose return pleases God. Here is he who answers the calling of the Lord without questions, follows him, and radically changes his life, thinking, and actions.

How relatable was the apostle Matthew to St. Augustine; how well did he understand Levi's joy of meeting the Lord and his desire to make a great feast for him; how clear to him were the words of the evangelist saying that Matthew "left everything." More than simply surrendering one's wealth, this means abandoning one's former habits, harmful routines, and mistreatment of others.

Will we be blessed with the grace of encountering the Lord, of hearing his sweet voice, of leaving that which gives us apparent happiness but really enslaves us? Or, rather, will we stand with the allegedly just Pharisees and say: "We are the chosen few, the believers, we truly need no change"?

Let us ask the Lord, through St. Matthew and St. Augustine, that we might be able to see Jesus passing by us in our daily lives, so that with his help we may pick ourselves up from where we fell and follow him. The Lord will truly rejoice at our return.

[6] *Confessions* 8.3.6 (189).

5

"Beset by temptations I struggle every day"

—*Confessions* 10.31.47

❑ ❑ ❑

No one needs to be convinced about the existence of countless temptations in our everyday lives. They have accompanied us since our childhood, since the very first moment we feel the urge to do something that we know is forbidden. One is so tempted to try this or that, because, after all, what could be wrong with it? New temptations appear throughout the years—new dangers, often in very subtle forms, coated with appealing beauty. We succumb to some and resist others. And today? No man can say he is free from temptation. We have been through much in life, we have learned from our own and others' mistakes, and yet time and time again we still encounter new perils—even in forms as familiar and basic as food and drink.

"Beset by . . . temptations I struggle every day against gluttony, for eating and drinking are not something I can decide to cut away once and for all, and never touch again, as I have been able to do with sexual indulgence. The reins that control the throat must therefore be relaxed or tightened judiciously; and is there anyone, Lord, who is not sometimes dragged a little beyond the bounds of what is needful? If there is such a person, he is a great man, so let him tell out the greatness of your name. I am not he, for I am a sinful man, yet I will tell out the greatness of your name nonetheless; and may he who has overcome the world intercede for my sins, and count me among the frailer members of his body, because your eyes rest upon my imperfections and in your book everyone will find a place."[7]

Temptation is also the theme of today's gospel reading, but in this case the stakes are immeasurably higher—here, the God-Man himself is tempted by Satan: "If you are the Son of God, command these stones to become loaves of bread" (Matt 4:3). Satan tempts Jesus with the ordinary, an everyday necessity for any living creature. He knew the Savior had been fasting for forty days and forty nights; he was hungry and thirsty, so why not follow the advice and satisfy the most basic of human needs? But Jesus answered him: "One does not live by bread alone, but by every word that comes from the mouth of God" (Matt 4:4). There are things more important in life than food and drink.

"Beset by . . . temptations I struggle every day against gluttony," St. Augustine honestly admits in his *Confessions*. Even our Lord Savior was subject to temptations, so why should we be immune? Fasting is not a popular idea in today's world—neither the word itself, nor its practice and spiritual motivation. We prefer to talk about *dieting* in all its shapes and forms. However, it is precisely during Lent when we should return to it and attempt even a minor sacrifice. This must be done for spiritual reasons, though, and not just to lose another six pounds and get slimmer. Rather, we seek to beautify our *souls* through even the smallest of sacrifices. This form of spiritual exercise will make it easier to face more serious temptations in other areas of our lives.

[7] *Confessions* 10.31.47 (268).

6

"Through loving humility
we find our way back to you"

—*Confessions* 3.8.15

❑ ❑ ❑

A few days ago, on Ash Wednesday, we heard our priests proclaim: "Repent, and believe in the Gospel" (Mark 1:15) or "Remember that you are dust, and to dust you shall return" (Gen 3:19) as they imposed ashes on our foreheads. The former comes from the Gospel of Mark, which is read on this First Sunday of Lent.

"Repent"—that is the encouragement God continually directs at us. We have all pondered it many times in the course of our lives—what it means in practice and how to answer it. One could say that it means a spiritual "turnaround," or a radical change in the direction of our spiritual journey.

Saint Augustine frequently meditated on the words of today's reading of the gospel, trying to understand the conversion he personally experienced and tell others about it. Years later, he wrote:

"[A man ridden with pride] in self-sufficient arrogance chooses to love a part of [the whole] only, a bogus 'one.' Yet through loving humility we find our way back to you. You purify our evil dispositions; you are merciful toward the sins of those who confess to you; you hear the groans of captives and set us free from the bonds we have forged for ourselves, provided only we no longer defy you in the arrogance of a spurious freedom, greedy to have more and thereby incurring the loss of everything, loving some advantage of our own better than yourself, who are the good of all."[8]

Repenting can be understood, interpreted, and explained in many ways. Saint Augustine teaches us today, in just a few words, that it can be done only through humility and piety.

We have no humility when we think ourselves better and more worthy of respect than others. We are humble when we hide our accomplishments and highlight the successes of others. At least once in life, every one of us has met someone famous, well-known, or wealthy who surprised us with his or her simplicity of manner, respect for others, gentleness that enraptured our heart, or faith that delighted our soul. "How humble a person!" we thought then and wanted to follow that example. But life has shown us, time and time again, that good intentions alone are not enough.

Encouraged by the example of Augustine and his words of humility as the way to repentance, let us this Lent closely observe Jesus, follow his actions, and listen to his words. How respectful is he to those around him, no matter their background or their past! We must learn from him who is "gentle and humble in heart" (Matt 11:29) the proper way to act and treat those we meet in our everyday lives.

[8] *Confessions* 3.8.15 (86–87).

7

"You, Lord, are immortal and without sin"

—*Confessions* 10.42.67

▢ ▢ ▢

Jesus is tempted by the devil in the desert. The Enemy is intelligent and exploits his hunger and thirst, starting with the suggestion of turning stones into bread. Later he shows him all the kingdoms of earth and promises power over them, but under the condition that Jesus worships Satan. And finally he proposes that Jesus cast himself from the pinnacle of the temple, since it was written that angels would save him.

Every time we read this passage, we feel as if we were present beside Jesus to witness the event. It is so not only because of the dramatic tension of the passage, but because we have experienced moments like these in our own lives.

Today's reading from the gospel, the words of our Savior himself, "Worship the Lord your God, and serve only Him" (Luke 4:8), must have been especially dear to St. Augustine. In his childhood and adolescence he often surrendered to instigations of him whom he calls the false mediator, and it took him a long time to understand the error of his ways and the necessity of God's grace in salvation.

"You, Lord, . . . are immortal and without sin. What we needed was a mediator to stand between God and men who should be in one respect like God, in another kin to human beings,

13

for if he were manlike in both regards he would be far from God, but if Godlike in both, far from us; and then he would be no mediator. By the same token that spurious mediator, by whose means pride was deservedly duped in keeping with your secret decree, does have one thing in common with human beings, namely sin."[9]

It may be slightly surprising for us that Jesus allowed Satan to confront him so directly, that he submitted himself to such trials. He probably wanted to show that he had experienced everything in life except sin and provide us with an example of how to overcome temptation in our everyday lives.

But then a thought pops into our minds—that Jesus is, after all, God, and our strength in fighting evil is not equal to his. That was also the thinking of St. Augustine, who on one hand relentlessly pursued happiness in his life and on the other acquiesced to temptations and passions that led him away from his goal.

It was the great tragedy of his life, one that we all share in various degrees. We all face temptations that we are unable to escape completely, but we must strive to overcome them. Lent is a time of reflecting on the weaknesses and roots of evil to which we all succumb. It is in those tasks that we must especially ask for God's help, so that we can shout out a strong "No!" to Satan and a strong "Yes!" to Christ, who is immortal and without sin.

[9] *Confessions* 10.42.67 (281–82).

8

"Is this boyhood innocence?"

—*Confessions* 1.7.11

❑ ❑ ❑

Saint Augustine remembers his childhood and his peers with fondness. In his *Confessions*, however, he does not conceal those examples of youth behavior that exhibit his tendency to evil. Much like we see today, Augustine's environment played a crucial role in the shaping of his young mind. It was governed by a set of rules and imposed a model of behavior on even the youngest members of society. From the earliest years, children were taught unhealthy rivalry and the pursuit of fame.

"I tell you this, my God, and confess to you those efforts for which I was praised; for at that time I believed that living a good life consisted in winning the favor of those who commended me. I failed to recognize the whirlpool of disgraceful conduct into which I had been flung, out of your sight. What could have been fouler in your eyes at that time than myself? . . . [In] games I would often seek to dominate by fraudulent means, because I was myself dominated by a vain urge to excel. And what was it that I was so unwilling to excuse, what did I so fiercely condemn if I detected it in others, but the very cheating I practiced myself? If I was caught out and accused of cheating I was more apt to lose my temper than to admit it. Is this boyhood innocence? No, Lord, it is not; hear me, dear God, it is not. . . . In spite of all this, O Lord our God, I give thanks to you, the most perfect, most good creator and ruler of the universe, and I would still thank you even if you had not willed me to live beyond boyhood. Even then I existed, I lived and I experienced; I took good care to keep myself whole and sound and so preserve the trace in me of your profoundly mysterious unity, from which I came."[10]

Saint Augustine presents a very sober assessment of his childhood. He gives thanks to God for those years, but while many others have idealized them and talked about the absolute innocence of children, he depicts the pollution of human nature stemming from original sin and strongly claims that the innocence of infants derives from the fragility of their frames, not innocence of their souls. He adds: "I have watched and experienced for myself the jealousy of a small child: he could not even speak, yet he glared with livid fury at his fellow-nursling."[11]

That is why St. Augustine advises anyone who reflects on his or her infancy and childhood to look first and foremost for signs of God's presence and goodness. There is, after all, something we observe in children that we cannot so easily see in adults: there is greater honesty and trust in people they meet and observe, a different outlook on the world around them. It is not surprising, then, that Jesus Christ, who knew the hearts of children, not only never spoke ill of them, but praised and invited them to Himself. "Let the little children come to me; do not stop them; for it is to such as these that the kingdom of God belongs" (Mark 10:14).

---

[10] *Confessions* 1.19.30–20.31 (59–60).
[11] Ibid., 1.7.11 (46).

9

"I continued to wander far from you"

—*Confessions* 2.1.1

□ □ □

Saint Augustine begins the second book of his *Confessions* with a reminiscence of his adolescence. He sees numerous mistakes he has made and the sad consequences of succumbing to passion, both of which appeared in his life with increased intensity at that time. The talented youth spent the sixteenth year of his life searching for the meaning of life amid the indulgence of sensual pleasures. His family's financial hardships forced him to discontinue his education. With so much free time on his hands, he spent most of it in bad company. His father was preoccupied with acquiring funds for Augustine's further education, while his pious mother Monica, concerned with her son's upbringing, could not shield him from the negative influence of his environment. Years later, St. Augustine described this stage of his life in the following way:

"There was a time in adolescence when I was afire to take my fill of hell. I boldly thrust out rank, luxuriant growth in various furtive love affairs; my beauty wasted away and I rotted in your sight, intent on pleasing myself and winning favor in the eyes of men. . . . I was flung hither and thither, I poured myself out, frothed and floundered in the tumultuous sea of my fornications; and you were silent. O my joy, how long I took to find you! At that time you kept silence as I continued to wander far from you and sowed more and more sterile seeds to my own grief, abased by my pride and wearied by my restlessness."[12]

Saint Augustine's openness in confessing his weaknesses, the painful honesty about this period of his life, when everything that was beautiful in him rotted to the core, is surprising. On one side we see a silent God, but on the other we see Augustine turning his back on God and wandering ever further away.

How close these words are to our own experiences and events from the lives of the followers of Christ everywhere! There are different kinds of abandoning from God: the sensational, when someone publicly, perhaps proudly, leaves the community of the faithful; and the private, focused more on internal life than spectacular gestures. It usually starts with a single matter or event in which we have shown poor vigilance or overconfidence. We forget that we are a whole composed of many parts, and even the smallest unfaithfulness influences all of our being and causes suffering. We have no control over what transpired in our past, but our spiritual history can and should serve as a lesson. It may even become a treasure, if we do not fail to see in it a silent, great, and loving presence of God, who tells us in today's reading of the gospel to call him our Father and who, in a truly mysterious way, allows people to wander away from him yet never ceases to wait for their return.

[12] *Confessions* 2.1.1–2.2 (62–63).

10

"You who uses pain to make your will known to us"

—*Confessions* 2.2.4

☐ ☐ ☐

We stay today with the sixteen-year-old Augustine, wandering away from God and suffering ever more greatly. According to the *Confessions*, it was at that time when Augustine, an intelligent and bright observer of life, began to ponder human suffering, its sources, and its meaning for human life. As an adult he would revisit that theme from a multitude of perspectives and under different circumstances during his literary and pastoral career. We may find great value in reading the reminiscence of his first deliberations on the topic—a matter that is not alien to any of us and is, in different degrees, a part of our lives from the very beginnings of our existence until our deathbeds.

"I went with the flood-tide of my nature and abandoned you. I swept across all your laws, but I did not escape your chastisements, for what mortal can do that? You were ever present to me, mercifully angry, sprinkling very bitter disappointments over all my unlawful pleasures so that I might seek a pleasure free from all disappointment. If only I could have done that, I would have found nothing but yourself, Lord, nothing but you yourself who use pain to make your will known to us, and strike only to heal, and even kill us lest we die away from you. Where was I, and how far was I exiled from the joys of your house in that sixteenth year of my bodily age, when the frenzy of lust imposed its rule on me, and I wholeheartedly yielded to it? A lust it was licensed by disgraceful human custom, but illicit before your laws."[13]

"Lord, . . . who use pain to make your will known to us, and strike only to heal." This simple and succinct statement illustrates the relationship between turning away from God and suffering. But this alone is not enough, since the suffering we experience is not always a consequence of our own weaknesses, sins, and shortcomings. Questions like "Why me?" and "Why does this misfortune happen to my family?" are ever-present in our lives and will forever remain, at least in some degree, without answer. Both believers and atheists alike experience suffering, but the former are able to see a different meaning in it. From their spiritual standpoint, there is not a single tear without meaning, no pain that is pointless, no suffering that is worthless.

Sister Grażyna Wojnowska, a Pallottine and missionary to Africa, in her poem "Mystery" writes the following:

> mystery locked away under key
>
> suffering without doors and windows
>
> no reason or result
>
> visible to the human eye
>
> only bathed in faith
>
> it glows strung up on a cross
>
> and if not subject to Love
>
> it will be hidden behind a bronze lock.[14]

---

[13] *Confessions* 2.2.4 (64).
[14] *Wszystko w życiu jest ważne* (Mielec, Poland: Poligraficzny Mielce, 2009), 38.

11

"Anyone would have heaped praise upon my father"

—*Confessions* 2.3.5

❑ ❑ ❑

Experts in spiritual life and psychology of religion state that the image of God the Father we perceive is influenced, at least to a certain degree, by our earthly father's character, behavior, and attitude toward us. This influence is especially significant in childhood and adolescence, when one starts to form opinions on life, the world, vocation, and God.

In the case of St. Augustine, we often refer to the role of his mother, St. Monica, in his life and conversion. His father, to whom the bishop of Hippo devotes significant attention in *Confessions*, is mentioned rarely.

"At the time I speak of anyone would have heaped praise upon my father, a man prepared to go beyond his means in spending as much money as was needed to send his son away to study, even in a distant city. No such efforts were made on behalf of the children of many other citizens who were far richer; yet all the while this same father of mine was unconcerned about how I would grow up for you, and cared little that I should be chaste, provided I was intellectually cultivated. It would be truer to say

21

that I was left fallow of your cultivation, O God, who are the only true and good owner of your field, my heart."[15]

Augustine describes his father not without criticism, yet at the time of writing the *Confessions* he already had a completely different view on his childhood, adolescence, and his parents. He values only that which helps him develop spiritually and come closer to God. Everything else, however useful, is pushed aside.

When pondering the words of St. Augustine, our thoughts gravitate spontaneously toward our own earthly fathers and the role they played in our lives, especially in the early years. They too were concerned about the financial well-being of the family, often more so than our mothers. Because of that they tended to be away from home more often and thus less familiar, sometimes even seeming mysterious. We longed for their return every time and wanted them to stay longer this time, despite their tendency to strictness.

Every family's story and every relationship between a parent and a child is different. A famous Polish director, Krzysztof Kieślowski, whose father passed away of tuberculosis at the age of 47, recalled that the presence of his dead father was as important to his work as the company of his living mother.

In today's reading of the gospel, Christ talks about his Father. It is a special relationship, unlike any other. And yet the words "If you then, who are evil, know how to give good gifts to your children, how much more will your Father in heaven give good things to those who ask him!" (Matt 7:11) relate, at least in some degree, to both kinds of fatherly love: the imperfect, earthly love and the one true Love that flows from the God in heaven.

On this day, let us commend our earthly fathers, both living and passed away, to God through St. Augustine. For they radiate their fatherhood upon us both during their lifetimes and after death.

---

[15] *Confessions* 2.3.5 (65).

12

"We derived pleasure from the deed simply because it was forbidden"

—*Confessions* 2.4.9

❏ ❏ ❏

It is sometimes said that St. Augustine was overly critical about the sins of his youth when writing the *Confessions* and that in reality he was guilty of no greater evil than his counterparts. There is truth in this, for sure, for we have to be able to discern the facts and events from their later assessment. Augustine portrays himself in the *Confessions* with a specific aim in mind—he wants to convey a certain spiritual message to his readers. To that end he looks at the events from his past in a particular light and analyzes them as a radically changed man, constantly making progress in his journey toward sainthood. Let us look at an example that perhaps at first glance seems trivial: a description of a theft in his childhood.

"Close to our vineyard there was a pear tree laden with fruit. This fruit was not enticing, either in appearance or in flavor. We nasty lads went there to shake down the fruit and carry it off at dead of night, after prolonging our games out-of-doors until that late hour according to our abominable custom. We took enormous quantities, not to feast on ourselves but perhaps to throw to the pigs; we did eat a few, but that was not our motive: we derived pleasure from the deed simply because it was forbidden."[16]

That is the experience of a sixteen-year-old Augustine, similar to many such events in the lives of youth in any historical and geographical context. There was, however, something special in it to which he returns thirty years later—the ever-present question, "Why did I do it?" Surely not because of hunger or the taste of pears. No, the desire to commit that which is forbidden was the reason. Another question then arises: how is it that evil's own attraction can lead us astray? "The malice was loathsome, and I loved it. I was in love with my own ruin, in love with decay: not with the thing for which I was falling into decay but with decay itself."[17]

To answer such a fundamental question, Augustine-the-theologian gives way to Augustine-the-philosopher, who writes about the significance of our will and the destructive charm of possessions, earthly distinctions, power, and sovereignty over others. Through the excessive love of such things one abandons things far more valuable and wanders away from the ultimate Good—that is, God.

It required a long process of cleansing for St. Augustine to be able to look back at the theft of pears, a symbol of disordered desires, from a different perspective and calmly ask: "How can I repay the Lord for my ability to recall these things without fear?"[18]

Augustine helps us to understand how even the smallest events from our lives, if properly analyzed and assessed, can teach us a great and fundamental lesson about rejecting evil and choosing good.

---

[16] *Confessions* 2.4.9 (67–68).
[17] Ibid., 2.4.9 (68).
[18] Ibid., 2.7.15 (72).

13

"Goodness from which kind actions spring"

—*Confessions* 10.33.50

❏ ❏ ❏

Both in St. Augustine's *Confessions* and in real life, history is intertwined with the present. Memories are a treasure, but from the spiritual and moral perspective the present is far more important. Augustine therefore asks himself: What is the current state of my soul? What is the main source of my anxiety and the obstacles in strengthening the friendship with God? After analyzing his inner world of thoughts, experiences, desires, and ideas, he concludes that there is still a great deal to be done in these areas and that in many ways he remains as he was in the past. He is not sure what to do about it, so a grown and strong man begins to weep for himself and encourages his followers to cry with him, for they do not do enough good.

"When . . . it happens that the singing has a more powerful effect on me than the sense of what is sung, I confess my sin and my need of repentance, and then I would rather not hear any singer. Such is my condition: weep with me, and weep for me, you who feel within yourselves that goodness from which kind actions spring! Any of you who do not have these feelings will not be moved by my experience. But do you hear me, O Lord my God: look upon me and see, have mercy and heal me, for in your eyes I have become an enigma to myself, and herein lies my sickness."[19]

What is the nature of our sickness? Following the example of the bishop of Hippo, we must ask ourselves this question, and Lent provides an excellent opportunity to do so. After taking the time to think, each and every one of us could give a different answer to that question, because just as each of our roads to God are different, so are the flaws that Augustine calls sicknesses. They all have one common denominator—a shortage of good deeds in an area of life that we have neglected for one reason or another. It could be an excessive attachment to material possessions, overly developed drive for success and fame, jealousy toward those better off, or a disorderly sphere of ideas and desires.

One of my friends sent me an e-mail with the following subject: "Ten questions that God will not ask." Some of them are, in my opinion, a good interpretation of St. Augustine's work. "God will not ask you how big your house was, but how many people you had let stay under your roof. God will not ask you how much you had earned, but if and what compromises you had made to get that money. God will not ask you what titles you had acquired, but if you had done your work honestly and to the utmost of your abilities. God will not ask you how many friends you had, but how many people had chosen you as a friend. God will not ask you. . . ." We could ask many such questions ourselves, but they all revolve around, in the words of St. Augustine, the goodness from which kind actions spring.

---

[19] *Confessions* 10.33.50 (270).

14

"Beauty which transcends all minds"

—Confessions 10.34.53

❑ ❑ ❑

Saint Augustine, being the sensitive man that he was, saw the many faces of beauty of this world. In his works he described the magnificence of the lands, seas, and creatures, who could all say: "We are beautiful." But as a philosopher he did not stop at noticing and depicting the beauty around him. No, he persistently asked *from whom* it comes and how beautiful must be the One who called to existence all of it. He thanked God for all beauty, because it leads us to him.

"O my God, for me you are loveliness itself; yet for all these things too I sing a hymn and offer a sacrifice of praise to you who sanctify me, because the beautiful designs that are born in our minds and find expression through clever hands derive from that Beauty which transcends all minds, the Beauty to which my own mind aspires day and night. Those who create beauty in material things, and those who seek it, draw from that source their power to appreciate beauty, but not the norm for its use. The norm is there, and could they but see it they would need to search no further. They could save their strength for you rather than dissipate it on enervating luxuries."[20]

[20] *Confessions* 10.34.53 (272).

Today's reading from the gospel talks about beauty of a very special nature. Three chosen apostles bear witness to an extraordinary event—the transfiguration of Jesus. They are blessed with the grace of viewing Jesus Christ's beauty in a mysterious way. Peter says to Him: "Lord, it is good for us to be here; if you wish, I will make three dwellings here" (Matt 17:4).

"What beauty will save the world?" asks Cardinal Martini. It is not enough to talk about the evil and ugliness of this world, not enough even to discuss justice, duty, common good, pastoral initiatives, or evangelical necessities. One must speak from a compassionate heart, experiencing the love that gives with joy and arouses fervor. One must praise the beauty of that which is true and just in life, for only that kind of beauty can open hearts and turn them toward God.[21]

After hearing today's reading of the gospel and reading the words of Augustine and Cardinal Martini, we can ask ourselves: Have we ever been blessed with a moment of clarity in seeing the beauty of God? Do we only see the human dimension, the sins, shortcomings, and scandals in the church, or do we also notice the presence of God, the ultimate Beauty, who invites and leads us to himself? What efforts do I undertake to make the worship I attend really beautiful and similar to the wonderful experience shared by the apostles on Mount Tabor?

Saint Augustine understood the unique beauty of experiencing proper human relationships, which require sacrifices, understanding, and forgiveness. Are we able to revel in the beauty of reconciliation between brothers and sisters and, through that, with God? Those and similar questions should encourage us to reflect upon the beauty in our lives. Furthermore, let them strengthen our belief that through the opening of our hearts to the beauty of God and his creation we may not only venerate him but also love, and thus in a way cocreate, everything that came from him.

---

[21] Carlo Maria Martini, *Saving Beauty: Cardinal Martini's Vision for the New Millenium* (London: St. Pauls, 2000), 12–13.

15

"Higher still we mounted"

—*Confessions* 9.10.24

❑ ❑ ❑

Life does not spare us hardship and worry. Sometimes it exhausts our physical and spiritual strength to the point that we can no longer perform everyday duties. We feel disheartened to do things that not long before were a source of joy. Moreover, we feel that God is distant and uninterested in our affairs.

Sometimes, however, the opposite happens: we unexpectedly notice clearly the presence of God and his love. In such times we completely forget our problems and are transported to a different world. We lack words to describe the experience, but we know that we have been given a special grace.

That was the case of the three apostles whom Jesus took to Mount Tabor: "And he was transfigured before them, and his clothes became dazzling white, such as no one on earth could bleach them" (Mark 9:2-3). Peter did not fully comprehend what transpired, but he was so filled with happiness he said: "Rabbi, it is good for us to be here" (Mark 9:5).

Saint Augustine experienced similar moments in his rich spiritual life, memories of which became important tools in overcoming life difficulties. One that we cannot fail to omit is the well-known conversation between him and his beloved mother Monica in Ostia.

"Step by step [we] traversed all bodily creatures and heaven itself, whence sun and moon and stars shed their light upon the earth. Higher still we mounted by inward thought and wondering discourse on your works, and we arrived at the summit of our own minds; and this too we transcended, to touch that land of never-failing plenty where you pasture Israel for ever with the food of truth. Life there is the Wisdom through whom all these things are made, and all others that have been or ever will be."[22]

The apostles experienced a unique kind of God's presence on Mount Tabor, as did St. Augustine and St. Monica in the garden of their house in Ostia. God can manifest his goodness and beauty anywhere he wishes, but it might not be a coincidence that he chooses places of special significance, sites that encourage thought and contemplation. It can happen to any of us when we least expect it. We just have to be mindful and not become swept away by the ceaseless flow of everyday life or become distracted by mass media. Sometimes it is enough to watch a sunset, sit on a bench in a beautiful park, or wonder at the sight of snowy mountain peaks. We might see that God changes his image before our eyes, that we see him in a new way, and that by letting him act in our lives we make room for God to transform and enrich our souls.

[22] *Confessions* 9.10.24 (227).

16

"O Lord my God, hear my prayer"

—*Confessions* 11.2.3

❑ ❑ ❑

The need for prayer in the life of any believer is self-evident. We can say it is as necessary for the spirit as food is for the body. Form, place, and setting for prayer, however, are much more complicated issues. Each one of us may have a different set of experiences and opinions on that matter.

In today's passage of the gospel we read: "Jesus took with him Peter and John and James, and went up on the mountain to pray. And while he was praying, the appearance of his face changed, and his clothes became dazzling white" (Luke 9:28-29).

Saint Augustine devotes a large portion of his *Confessions* to prayer, and he even includes some of his invocations to God. Below is a part of one of them:

> "O Lord my God, hear my prayer,
>
> may your mercy hearken to my longing,
>
> a longing on fire not for myself alone
>
> but to serve the brethren I dearly love;
>
> you see my heart and know this is true.
>
> Let me offer in sacrifice to you the service of my heart
> and tongue,
>
> but grant me first what I can offer you;

> for I am needy and poor,
>
> but you are rich unto all who call upon you,
>
> and you care for us though no care troubles you.
>
> Circumcise all that is within me from presumption
>
> and my lips without from falsehood."[23]

Distinct stages are visible in this prayer of the bishop of Hippo. First, he asks God to hear his prayer and mentions his longing for the reality that is the focus of the beseeching prayer. He explains that it will not only serve himself but also his brethren. He then proceeds to confess the honesty of his appeal, which is well known to God. Augustine does not hide his weaknesses and praises God's goodness and generosity. Finally, he confesses the nature of his plea: he asks for freedom from falsehood, both in private and public official speech—that is, in teaching.

When contemplating the transfiguration of Jesus on Mount Tabor and the changing of his image on this Second Sunday of Lent, we ought to take a closer look at our own prayers in light of St. Augustine's prayer. Through it, we may open up to God, allowing him to transfigure our spirit by showing his divine nature and power. From our own observation and experience, we know that prayer can be difficult even for devout followers of Christ. But only through prayer may we learn to talk to God, be at peace, and reach true happiness. Saint Augustine adds: "We confess to you our miseries and the mercies you have shown us in your will to set us free completely, as you have begun to do already; and by so confessing to you we lay bare our loving devotion. Our hope is that we may cease to be miserable in ourselves and may find our beatitude in you."[24]

---

[23] *Confessions* 11.2.3 (285).
[24] Ibid., 11.1.1 (284).

17

"I blundered headlong into love"

—*Confessions* 3:1.1

□ □ □

A sixteen-year-old Augustine arrived at Carthage to continue his education. Right at the beginning of his stay he went through some morally distressing experiences, which he recalled and described in his *Confessions*. Not only does he present the facts but assesses their significance for his spiritual development.

"So I arrived at Carthage, where the din of scandalous love-affairs raged cauldron-like around me. I was not yet in love, but I was enamored with the idea of love. . . . I polluted the stream of friendship with my filthy desires and clouded its purity with hellish lusts; yet all the while, befouled and disgraced though I was, my boundless vanity made me long to appear elegant and sophisticated. I blundered headlong into the love which I hoped would hold me captive, but in your goodness, O my God, my mercy, you sprinkled bitter gall over my sweet pursuits. I was loved, and I secretly entered into an enjoyable liaison, but I was also trammeling myself with fetters of distress, laying myself open to the iron rods and burning scourges of jealousy and suspicion, of fear, anger and quarrels."[25]

---

[25] *Confessions* 3.1.1 (75–76).

Saint Augustine's painfully honest words leave no doubt that after an idle year in Thagaste, where he spent a good deal of time in bad company, he came to a big city and indulged his passions.

Some scholars have attempted, in vain, to justify the actions of the young man, claiming that he was yet unbaptized and acted in a way that was common among his peers. They claim that Augustine intentionally exaggerated his actions to better portray divine mercy. Yet the disorderly emotions and deeds of the young man should be neither exaggerated nor diminished—they were as they were. The author recalls them with sorrow and assesses them in a clearly negative way. First and foremost, he tries to be honest with God, himself, and the reader.

Objectively judging past experiences is not easy for anyone, especially in an area as sensitive as sexuality. It is a gift from God that requires special care, humility, and responsibility. Lent is a suitable time to take another look at this important aspect of our lives. In its assessment we too face the dangers of both exaggeration and whitewashing. Some people cannot jettison the heavy baggage of negative experiences weighing them down, even after years of trying. They can even believe that God has forgiven them, yet they cannot forgive themselves. Others follow the spirit and mentality of our times and fail to notice their own evil and disgrace, however serious it might be.

Let St. Augustine, who once succumbed to passions but could later believe in the mercy of God, beseech Christ on our behalf, so that he may bless us with the graces that we need to properly assess and experience our sexuality.

18

"I relished the freedom of a runaway"

—*Confessions* 3.3.5

❑ ❑ ❑

During his time in Carthage, young Augustine diligently studied rhetoric, seeing it more as a way to find true happiness than a future source of income. The more he indulged in his passions, the stronger he felt the need to search for something more lasting in life. He avidly frequented the theater and was often moved by the plays he watched. The misery of the characters resonated with his own, and he often found himself deeply moved during the shows, with tears rolling down his cheeks. Full of contradicting emotions, he could not understand what was happening to him.

"It led me to . . . plunge into treacherous abysses, into depths of unbelief and a delusive allegiance to demons, to whom I was offering my evil deeds in sacrifice. And in all these sins your scourges beat upon me. Even within the walls of your church, during the celebration of your sacred mysteries, I once made bold to indulge in carnal desire and conduct that could yield only a harvest of death; and for this you struck me with severe punishments, though none that matched my guilt. O my God, you were immensely merciful to me, and were my refuge from the terrible dangers amid which I wandered, head held high. I withdrew further and further from you, loving my own ways and not yours, relishing the freedom of a runaway slave."[26]

This is also the image of a modern man who often plunges into the depths of unbelief, surprised by the advancement of technology, speed of information flow, and ruthless competition. He is lost in the maze of everyday life, and he starts to wander aimlessly but wants to do so with his head held up high. He does not confess his sin and goes further and further away from God. And if he also carries the heavy burden of past sins, he is in danger of becoming a fugitive. That was the case of Cain, the murderer of his brother Abel, who heard God say: "When you till the ground, it will no longer yield to you its strength; you will be a fugitive and a wanderer on the earth" (Gen 4:12).

But the Lord did not give us life so that we would suffer endlessly. No! The church reminds us of that during Lent and shows us the way to get rid of the heavy burden of past sins, to free ourselves from underneath the crushing weight, and, most important, to believe in the God who is almighty and merciful. We read in the Book of Isaiah: "though your sins are like scarlet, they shall be like snow; though they are red like crimson, they shall become like wool" (Isa 1:18).

Let those words, which became reality in the life and spiritual transformation of St. Augustine, help us abandon the freedom of a fugitive and come closer to the kind of freedom shared by those who have trust in the Lord.

[26] *Confessions* 3.3.5 (78).

19

"All my hollow hopes suddenly seemed worthless"

—*Confessions* 3.4.7

□ □ □

Augustine, although engulfed by passions, did not stop searching for true happiness, and when during his studies of rhetoric he encountered an interesting work he analyzed it and tried to filter out ideas useful to him during his difficult life journey. One of them was Cicero's *Hortensius*, which encouraged readers to take up philosophy. Years later Augustine recalled it in the following way:

"The book changed my way of feeling and the character of my prayers to you, O Lord, for under its influence my petitions and desires altered. All my hollow hopes suddenly seemed worthless, and with unbelievable intensity my heart burned with longing for the immortality that wisdom seemed to promise. I began to rise up, in order to return to you. My interest in the book was not aroused by its usefulness in the honing of my verbal skills (which was supposed to be the object of the studies I was now pursuing, in my nineteenth year, at my mother's expense, since my father had died two years earlier); no, it was not merely as an instrument for sharpening my tongue that I used that book, for it had won me over not by its style but by what it had to say."[27]

[27] *Confessions* 3.4.7 (79).

While reading the work of the Roman orator, Augustine began to understand the mistakes he had made in life and his longing for true happiness intensified. Yet he encountered another obstacle: the philosophical relationship between faith and reason. At the time he believed the question should not be resolved with a complementary duality of faith and reason, but rather a choice between two alternatives: faith *or* reason. Therefore we can assume that Augustine, fascinated by some rational tendencies in the philosophy of the period, chose the latter: reason. For a time he became a follower not of the God who offers faith, but the god who taught him philosophy.

But his reading of *Hortensius* changed the way the nineteen-year-old Augustine thought and acted. First and foremost, he developed a new outlook on earthly ambitions, the pursuit of fame, and the immoral actions of his previous years. The work of Cicero spoke to him more through content than refined form, and he came to the conclusion that in life one must search for what is truly important. Yet Augustine's path to God was still to be long and winding.

As Pope Benedict XVI reflected, "St. Augustine was a man who never lived superficially; his thirst, his restless and constant thirst for the Truth is one of the basic characteristics of his existence; not however for 'pseudo-truths,' incapable of giving the heart lasting peace, but of that Truth that gives meaning to life and is the 'dwelling-place' in which the heart finds serenity and joy."[28]

---

[28] Pope Benedict XVI, General Audience, August 25, 2010.

20

"Love wisdom itself"

—*Confessions* 3.4.8

□ □ □

Reading Cicero's *Hortensius* intensified St. Augustine's desire to search for true, everlasting wisdom, the kind that leads to happiness. This drive manifests itself in every human being; the problem is that there truly are many different definitions of wisdom.

Cicero showed how humans from the very dawn of time tried to find a way to internal peace and satisfaction by observing the ever-changing and ephemeral nature of reality and inquiring into the seemingly unknown and mysterious ultimate destination.

After reading Cicero's work, Augustine was assured that there were—and still are—people who lead their followers astray under the pretense of promoting philosophy. Cicero pointed out and exposed them, confirming Augustine in the knowledge that the road to wisdom in life is bumpy, difficult, and full of mistakes, sacrifices, and failures.

Years later, when writing his *Confessions*, Augustine understood the significance of St. Paul's teachings and the truth of his words on philosophy, which he had not yet known at the time of reading *Hortensius*.

"One can . . . find an exposition of the salutary warning given by your Spirit through your good, devout servant: *Take care that no one deceives you with philosophy and empty, misleading ideas derived from man-made traditions, centered on the elemental spirits of this world and not on Christ; for in him all the fullness of the Godhead dwells in bodily wise.* At the time these words of the apostle were still unknown to me; but you know, O light of my heart, that there was one thing and one only that brought me joy in the exhortation to wisdom: that by its call I was aroused and kindled and set on fire to love and seek and capture and hold fast and strongly cling not to this or that school, but to wisdom itself, whatever it might be."[29]

Different are the paths that God offers the one searching for wisdom. Our road, as believers, is somewhat easier, but that does not mean that we may stop searching altogether. We are not free from the obstacles on the road to wisdom that stem from what the modern world offers—that is, achieving happiness through an easier and quicker path that requires less sacrifice. Above all, however, everywhere around us we can observe the attempts of attaining wisdom without God in any shape or form, without his creation, redemption, providence, or mercy. The words of the prophet Jeremiah resonate loudly in contrast: "Blessed are those who trust in the Lord, whose trust is the Lord" (Jer 17:7).

May St. Augustine and St. Paul save us from delusions based on human premise, and may they give us strength in the constant search for true Wisdom.

[29] *Confessions* 3.4.8 (79–80).

21

"I disdained to be a little child"

—*Confessions* 3.5.9

❑ ❑ ❑

Encouraged to look for true wisdom in life by studying the works of the ancient philosophers, Augustine began to read the Scriptures. He does not mention in the *Confessions* whether they were recommended to him or whether his reading began of his own initiative or the influence of childhood conversations with his beloved mother. What we do know is that he approached the Scriptures with the same attitude as the other works he studied up to that point—that is, more as a teacher than a student. He was therefore deeply disappointed with both the content and the form of the Scriptures. They were too enigmatic for him, and the style fell short of the refined elegance of classical texts.

"My approach then was quite different from the one I am suggesting now: when I studied the Bible and compared it with Cicero's dignified prose, it seem to me unworthy. My swollen pride recoiled from its style and my intelligence failed to penetrate to its inner meaning. Scripture is a reality that grows along with little children, but I disdained to be a little child and in my high and mighty arrogance regarded myself as grown-up."[30]

---

[30] *Confessions* 3.5.9 (80).

In this short and succinct passage, St. Augustine describes his attitude toward the Scriptures at the time of his first reading as "proud" and "arrogant." This pride prevented him from being the student of the Bible's Author. Although not able to comprehend much, a child instinctively trusts that its father knows and can do anything and is also certain of his love. During his first reading of the Scriptures, Augustine lacked this trust of a child, as did the religious leaders of the nation of Israel. In today's reading of the gospel, we hear the parable of the wicked tenants, followed by an account of the priests' reaction: "When the chief priests and the Pharisees heard his parables, they realized that he was speaking about them. They wanted to arrest him, but they feared the crowds, because they regarded him as a prophet" (Matt 21:45-46). Both Augustine and Jewish religious leaders alike lacked a child's attitude when reading or listening to inspired words, and so their proud and arrogant hearts could not be spiritually healed.

Various forms of pride, sometimes very sophisticated, can drown out the child of God in our souls. Let us ask St. Augustine to intercede on our behalf with the Lord, so that during Lent we may ponder on the word of God, rediscover our spiritual childhood, and through that come closer to our Lord.

22

"You were gentler still with him when he returned in his need"

—*Confessions* 1.18.28

❏ ❏ ❏

We have all read the parable of the Prodigal Son or, as it is sometimes called, the parable of the Merciful Father. We have pondered the behavior of both the elder and younger son, trying to understand which one of them better represents the nature of our own separation from God. Each time we might notice a new detail, a new element of this rich story, that can be of special significance to us and help us see more clearly the face of the ever-loving God.

Naturally, this parable was especially close to St. Augustine's heart. He mentions it often in the *Confessions*, as he shows its significance to himself, as well as that which might be especially useful to followers of Christ.

"Not with our feet or by traversing great distances do we journey away from you or find our way back. That younger son of yours in the gospel did not hire horses or carriages, nor did he board ships, nor take wing in any visible sense nor put one foot before the other when he journeyed to that far country where he could squander at will the wealth you, his gentle father, had given him at his departure. Gentle you were then, but gentler still with him when he returned in his need. No, to be estranged in a spirit of lust, and lost in its darkness, that is what it means to be far away from your face."[31]

There is no detailed exegesis of the parable in that fragment of St. Augustine's work, although elsewhere in the text he conducts a detailed analysis of single words from the Bible, certain expressions and their meanings, and the context behind a passage and its significance. Here, however, he seems to intentionally avoid it so as not to get lost in the details. The important message is: wandering away from God is not done physically or spatially, but spiritually and in one's heart.

We move away from God when we become slaves to passions that obstruct God's face. Those passions come in different forms. When analyzing his own departure from God, St. Augustine points to his desire for fame and the approval of others, present since his early years. In order to stand out from the crowd and win acclaim, especially with influential people, he was willing to lie, steal, and break rules.

That is only one example of departing from God, but a very meaningful one for us today. We are constantly tempted to win the approval of our teachers, employers, and peers. We might be ready to make seemingly small concessions in order to get that promotion we want, but with time our conscience begins to weigh us down. If we hear its voice, even if it is barely noticeable, it is a sign of God's presence with us. We must open our hearts for the goodness of the merciful Father, who never stops loving us but ever more longingly awaits our return.

[31] *Confessions* 1.18.28 (58).

23

"Let me not be my own life"

—*Confessions* 12.10.10

☐ ☐ ☐

Saint Augustine's spiritual history is primarily the story of his constant returning to God. It is revealing that the bishop of Hippo uses the present tense to address God in the *Confessions*, even though many years had passed since his conversion. In this way he emphasizes that a very special grace that was once bestowed upon him, one that allowed him to come out of the darkest night, was only the beginning of a long and ongoing process. He heard the voice of the Lord then, very soft and difficult to hear among other, stronger voices, urging him to go in a completely different direction. The words of the Lord were special—they came from the only One who could give Augustine his life back, for we cannot come back to life once left to our own devices.

"O Truth, illumination of my heart, let not my own darkness speak to me! I slid away to material things, sank into shadow, yet even there, even from there, I loved you. Away I wandered, yet I remembered you. I heard your voice behind me, calling me back, yet scarcely heard it for the tumult of the unquiet. See now, I come back to you, fevered and panting for your fountain. Let no one bar my way, let me drink it and draw life from it. Let me not be my own life: evil was the life I lived of myself; I was death to myself; but in you I begin to live again. Speak to me yourself, converse with me. I have believed your scriptures, but those words are full of hidden meaning."[32]

There is a clear reference to today's reading from St. John's gospel in which Jesus talks with a Samaritan woman about living water. Augustine talks about his yearning for a fountain of living water, and once he finds it he does not want to stop drinking.

Just like Augustine and the Samaritan woman at Jacob's well, we all look for that which can truly quench our thirst; we look for the living water that only God can provide. During Lent we must look for God ever more eagerly, listen to him more attentively, and recognize his will. If we fail to engage in that, we will instinctively look for something else to serve as a substitute. We see that in modern television, especially popular game shows, where among a flood of light everything appears colorful and life is shown as a chase of success—particularly the grand and unexpected kind that supposedly provides full and lasting happiness. But the game ends, the lights are turned off, and what is left is a void even greater than before. Others have won—we were just the audience.

Help us, Lord, to understand through the words of St. Augustine that we cannot bring ourselves back to life and that we cannot come back to you without aid. Help us open up to your love, which you once showed to the Samaritan woman and many others during your earthly travels.

---

[32] *Confessions* 12.10.10 (317–18).

24

"The heart has strayed from him"

—*Confessions* 4.12.18

❏ ❏ ❏

In his *Confessions*, St. Augustine repeatedly and in different situations states that God is ever present in the depths of our hearts. He underlines this truth for very obvious reasons: influenced, among other things, by Greek and Roman philosophy, he searched for God in the universe for many years, yet the Creator was always closer than he could ever have imagined. Augustine understood this fundamental error in his pursuits only when he opened his heart to the grace of the God who incessantly waited for his arrival.

"Let us love him, for he made these things and he is not far off, for he did not make them and then go away; they are from him but also in him. You know where he is, because you know where truth tastes sweet. He is most intimately present to the human heart, but the heart has strayed from him. Return to your heart, then, you wrongdoers, and hold fast to him who made you. Stand with him and you will stand firm, rest in him and you will find peace."[33]

---

[33] *Confessions* 4.12.18 (104).

Augustine's heart wandered the wilderness for years, and for years it did not know peace. Similar was the case of the merchants and money changers from today's gospel reading, although it took place at a different time. They departed from the true God; they did not understand the essence of religion. Furthermore, they tried to exploit people's devotion to religious matters for their own benefit. They saw the temple as a marketplace where one turns a profit and participates in dishonest transactions.

Both the passage from the gospel and the quote from the *Confessions* warn against people who are willing to sacrifice everything, including religion, for their own interest. They pay no heed to clear signs sent by God; they do not try to change their thinking nor reflect on their lives in any deeper way.

That is the image of a man so self-focused that he cannot open himself to redemptive truth. A prolonged period of wrongdoing causes habits and routines to form. Merchants and money changers from the temple probably saw nothing wrong in using a place of worship to conduct business. What a terrible mistake! It took Jesus' firm intervention to remind them and any onlookers of the proper hierarchy of values.

To a certain extent, we are all in danger of developing a wrong attitude to religion and the church, although it might not be in a form so acute as that of Augustine before his conversion—or that of the merchants in the temple. We succumb to the temptation of misusing religion when, for example, we use our church affiliation to obtain personal gain or flaunt our piety for others to see but then change our opinions and attitudes a moment later to protect our exposed yet cushy professional positions.

May Jesus help us during Lent to rid ourselves of everything that prohibits us from having a clear, unambiguous, and selfless attitude toward the church, which he established for our salvation.

25

"I contemplated them and was adread"

—*Confessions* 10.40.65

❑ ❑ ❑

God shows much patience toward his creation. Early Christian writers referred to this trait by its Latin name, *patientia*, and they touched upon it often, urging their readers to follow God's example in this respect. This advice is still current after long centuries, for today we may often see people getting anxious, running to and fro, glancing impatiently at their watches, or too quickly losing their tempers.

After his conversion, when St. Augustine carefully analyzed his past actions and the goodness and mercy calling him incessantly toward God, he praised God for his patience. He felt as if he was at school, where God himself was the teacher explaining the often complicated matters of life and happiness after which humans strive.

"O Truth, is there any road where you have not walked with me, teaching me what to avoid and what to aim at, whenever I referred to you the paltry insights I had managed to attain, and sought your guidance? I surveyed the external world as best I could with the aid of my senses, and studied the life my body derives from my spirit, and my senses themselves. Then I moved inward to the storehouse of my memory, to those vast, complex places amazingly filled with riches beyond counting; I contemplated them and was adread."[34]

In today's gospel we hear a story of a man who owned a fig tree that had not borne fruit for three years. He shared with a gardener his intention to cut the tree down, but the latter asked him to show patience and leave the tree for one more year. The gardener promised to dig around the tree and put manure on it—simply put, he wanted to create favorable conditions for bearing fruit. If the efforts proved to be in vain, then the tree would be cut down the following year.

Augustine knew how much he owed to the patience of God, who waited not three but many years for him to bear spiritual fruit. God closely followed the transformation of Augustine's soul, gave him the necessary means, shone light and put different people on his path, and spoke to him, through his mother Monica especially. Augustine finally opened up to God's mercy and started to bear the rich fruit of committed pastoral work, administering sacraments, teaching, and preaching. He left behind works that inspire many Christians to contemplate, search for God, and change their lives.

Are we able to read the signs that God directs at us when we do not bear the expected fruit? Are we able to use the time he gives us during Lent for prayer and making appropriate decisions, however small, in matters that we have been unable to change in the years past?

The patient God keeps us alive and constantly provides us with opportunities to turn toward him. May St. Augustine, who himself went through a complicated spiritual transformation, aid us in upholding that which is good, noble, and leads us to God.

[34] *Confessions* 10.40.65 (280).

26

"They told me lies about you"

—*Confessions* 3.6.10

❑ ❑ ❑

Augustine was not fascinated by his first reading of the Holy Bible, he was not spiritually moved or intellectually enlightened. There was still a void in his haughty mind and heart that he tried to fill in some way. In his search for wisdom he turned to the Manicheans, a rapidly spreading sect of the time. He had listened to them before, but later he deemed them trustworthy and decided to join their ranks. Years later he recalled that period of his life in the following way:

"They would say, 'Truth, truth!' and had plenty to tell me on the subject, but truth had no place in them. They told me lies not only about you, who are truly the Truth, but also about the elements of this world that is your creation. I ought to have gone beyond them and beyond what even truthful philosophers have taught out of love for you, my Father, who are the highest good and the loveliness in all lovely things."[35]

How could it be that such a bright young man was so enthralled by theories that he came to criticize vigorously later in life?

---

[35] *Confessions* 3.6.10 (81).

Augustine had believed that the Manicheans would lead him to discovering the truth and through that to true happiness. This is, after all, what he wanted above all else.

He was also drawn by the Manichean promises of achieving happiness through the means of reason, not faith. Augustine was already partial to rationalism in his philosophical studies for some time, so he readily accepted their arguments.

Furthermore, the Manicheans claimed that they were the true spiritual followers of Christ, liberated from the many alleged contradictions of the Old Testament. So Augustine believed that by moving away from the Catholic Church he was not abandoning Jesus Christ.

The Manicheans postulated a solution to the question of suffering by assuming that two eternal principles, good and evil, were locked in a constant conflict. Having striven to answer the question of the origin of evil since the very beginning of his philosophical pursuits, Augustine accepted this seemingly simple and logical explanation.

These theories are strangely similar to the reasons given by those abandoning the church today: only accepting that which can be empirically and rationally justified; breaking free from the allegedly restrictive norms of the church; a modern approach to the questions of evil, disease, disaster, and life in general.

Augustine went through a deep transformation and conversion; he even became a saint. But what about our brothers and sisters who leave today? What can we do for them? To paraphrase a poem by Fr. Jan Twardowski, we can tell them that we do not come to convert them and then confide in them our secret—that we want to trust God just like children do.

27

"By these stages I was led deeper into hell"

—*Confessions* 3:6.11

❏ ❏ ❏

Today we stay with that part of the *Confessions* in which Augustine recalls his time with the sect of the Manicheans. The reasoning of the group's members did not fully and deeply convince the young philosopher searching for truth but, seeing no other solution, he told himself that he would grow happier the more thoroughly he studied. In fact, however, he began feeling the exact opposite: the anxiety in his heart grew and at times led him to despair. He realized that it was still his senses and not his intellect that influenced his actions the most, despite the Manichean promises of finding happiness through purely rational means.

"By these stages I was led deeper into hell, laboring and chafing under the scarcity of truth, because I was seeking you, my God, not through that power of the mind by which you have chosen to rank me above the beasts, but only through carnal inclination. To you do I confess this, for you showed mercy to me before ever I could confess it. You were more intimately present to me than my innermost being, and higher than the highest peak of my spirit."[36]

[36] *Confessions* 3.6.11 (83).

Augustine required time and experience to realize that the road he had chosen led to nowhere. Above all he needed the light of God to see that he was going not toward but away from true happiness.

A similar story took place centuries before in Nazareth. We read about it in yesterday's reading from the Gospel of Luke. Jesus arrived at the city where he had spent his childhood and adolescence. When he accused the Jews gathered in the synagogue and their ancestors of a lack of faith, "all in the synagogue were filled with rage. They got up, drove him out of the town, and led him to the brow of the hill on which their town was built, so that they might hurl him off the cliff" (Luke 4:28-29).

The paradox of the situation is that God was very close to both Augustine the Manichean and the people of Nazareth, but they turned away from him. Those in the synagogue who listened to Jesus were given an unbelievable opportunity to hear the words of the Messiah whom they had awaited for centuries. But of course "no prophet is accepted in the prophet's hometown" (Luke 4:24). Augustine, on the other hand, had searched endlessly for God and failed to see him within his own soul. Only years later when he analyzed that experience could he confess to God: "You were more intimately present to me than my innermost being, and higher than the highest peak of my spirit."[37]

Let us pray that through St. Augustine, during Lent and beyond, we may see how unique is each day, encounter, and situation, and above all may we see God's presence in them, for he is closer to us than it may seem.

---

[37] Ibid., 3.6.11 (83).

28

"This is what happens when anyone abandons you"

—*Confessions* 3.8.16

❏ ❏ ❏

While recalling and analyzing the period of fascination with Manichaeism in his life, Augustine portrayed the negative attitudes he saw in people around him at that time. Years later, when he looked back on his past experiences, he concluded that some failings are especially detrimental to spiritual growth, regardless of one's faith and convictions. They are dangerous because they are the reason behind many sinful actions, unjust accusations, and immoral practices. Envy and satisfaction at another's misery, so familiar to some people, are chief among them.

In his *Confessions* Augustine states that envy manifests itself "when a person in wretched circumstances envies one more fortunate, or one who is successful in an enterprise jealously injures another because he fears the other will catch up with him, or is chagrined because that person already has. Or it may simply be pleasure in the misfortunes of others that tempts people to crime: this is the pleasure felt by those who watch gladiators, and anyone who laughs at and mocks other people. . . . This is what happens when anyone abandons you, the fountain of life, the One, the true creator and ruler of the universe."[38]

It is interesting to note that although Augustine wrote this passage after his conversion and mainly about his past, he used the present tense—perhaps to show that the danger of which he speaks is still current, affecting believers and nonbelievers alike. Envy was an integral part of the human experience since time immemorial, as evidenced by the tragic story of two brothers in Genesis: Cain and Abel. Envy can lead to the most despicable of crimes; it gives birth to hate, spitefulness, happiness at the misery of others, and disappointment at their successes.

We all wish this was not our reality. We are, after all, believers, but we realize that we succumb to many different kinds of envy. The brother of the Prodigal Son could not find it in himself to be happy about his kin returning home. When we cannot feel joy at our neighbor's better health, bigger bank account, and greater recognition or popularity, we are like that son who never physically left his family homestead but became so spiritually distant. We too are not truly home when we do not stand up to defend the wrongly accused, even if nothing has been proven yet, and feel somewhat satisfied because of their predicament, because they were too well off thus far.

Let us pray that through the intercession of St. Augustine we may overcome our resentments of others, our envious thoughts and attitudes, and our rivalry and suspicions, and in doing so may we come back to the Father of true love who is waiting for us.

[38] *Confessions* 3.8.16 (86–87).

29

"My mother was weeping for me"

—Confessions 3.11.19

❑ ❑ ❑

Augustine's mother, St. Monica, was raised in a Christian household and then married off to Patricius, a pagan and violent man, yet one respectful toward his wife. She influenced him more with the goodness of her heart, patience, and gentleness than anything else. With her conduct and fervent prayer, she obtained from God the grace of conversion for her husband. Patricius was baptized toward the end of his life. But she wept more for one of her sons, the highly talented Augustine who unfortunately had led a very dissolute life.

Later, after his conversion, when the bishop of Hippo recalled his spiritual journey and the role of his mother in it, he put it in words that would compose a literary classic, touching the hearts even of those with completely different convictions.

"You stretched out your hand from on high and pulled my soul out of these murky depths because my mother, who was faithful to you, was weeping for me more bitterly than ever mothers wept for the bodily death of their children. In her faith and in the spiritual discernment she possessed by your gift she regarded me as dead; and you heard her, O Lord, you heard her and did not scorn those tears of hers which gushed forth and watered the ground beneath her eyes wherever she prayed. Yes, you did indeed hear her."[39]

Parents are not ashamed of tears profusely shed when they ask for the well-being of their beloved children. It is indeed hard to imagine how many tears Monica wept for her son, since according to him she wept more bitterly than other mothers do for the death of their children. Although she thought fervent prayer was the best way to reach the desired goal—the conversion of her son—she did not stop there. On one occasion she brought her problem to a pious bishop to implore him to speak with Augustine and show him the error of his ways. He replied, however, that the youth was not old enough to listen to cautions. Monica insisted, but the bishop told her that he also had been given to the Manicheans to be fostered in his youth by his own ill-informed mother. Only in time did he come to understand that he should leave the sect, but that too did not convince Monica, who wished for her son to amend his behavior without delay. Still weeping, she begged the bishop to meet with Augustine. Somewhat impatiently, the bishop replied: "Go away now; but hold on to this: it is inconceivable that he should perish, a son of tears like yours."[40]

Let us offer our thanks to God today, through St. Monica and St. Augustine, for the tears of our mothers shed from concern for our well-being and for their prayers and hardship in fostering our spiritual growth.

[39] *Confessions* 3.11.19 (89).
[40] *Confessions* 3.12.21 (91).

30

"We pursued the contest for ephemeral wreaths"

—*Confessions* 4.1.1

◻ ◻ ◻

At the beginning of the fourth book of his *Confessions* Augustine once again recalls his youth. In particular he blames himself for two major faults during his time teaching grammar and rhetoric in Thagaste and Carthage: vanity and his association with the Manichean sect. Augustine does not try to justify his actions but rather attempts to understand the processes that led him to make such wrong choices and bad decisions. He also wants to be direct about his past, find the reasons behind his attitudes toward the world around him at the time, and describe the desires that he had pursued.

"Throughout those nine years, from my nineteenth to my twenty-eighth year, I and others like me were seduced and se-ducers, deceived ourselves and deceivers of others amid a wel-ter of desires: publicly through the arts reputed 'liberal,' and secretly under the false name of religion. In the one we were arrogant, in the other superstitious, and in both futile; under the auspices of the former we pursued trumpery popular ac-claim, theatrical plaudits, song-competitions and the contest for ephemeral wreaths, we watched trashy shows and indulged our intemperate lusts."[41]

---

[41] *Confessions* 4.1.1 (92).

Confusion, deceit, ambition, pursuing empty fame—these are only some of the effects of young Augustine's vanity, living in a decayed society, and being unable to break free from it. He later portrayed it vividly as a contest for "ephemeral wreaths."

Everyone needs to feel understood by others, and everyone wants to display the skills, accomplishments, and the proper application of talents with which he or she has been blessed. There is nothing improper about that. Problems arise when the pursuit of acclaim and success becomes the main goal of our actions, and it is even worse when for the sake of success we apply methods contradicting the Great Commandment to love our neighbors as ourselves.

Each and every one of those who reflect on their lives during Lent can easily point to those times when unhealthy ambitions and rivalries and the need to flaunt superiority or excessive pursuit of reputation surfaced more than usual. It might be difficult for us today to believe that we, in fact, acted in this way out of ill-directed desires and wasted the time that was given to us. In the words of Dag Hammarskjöld:

> But in the meantime how grievous the memory
> Of hours frittered away.[42]

We beseech you, Lord, to grant us through St. Augustine the ability to feel regret over the mistakes of our lives and to listen attentively to your words, so that through our actions we may deserve the wreaths that never wither away.

[42] Dag Hammarskjöld, *Markings*, trans. Leif Sjöberg and W. H. Auden (New York: Knopf, 1964), 6.

31

"Forgive her any debts"

—*Confessions* 9.13.35

▢ ▢ ▢

It is said that St. John Vianney once asked one of his fellow priests who complained about his uncooperative flock: "Do you pray for them, Father?"

We pray for those who are entrusted to our spiritual care, but we often do it without conviction. We might even occasionally feel doubt about the effectiveness of our prayers on behalf of those who do not believe in God or are indifferent about religion. Simply put, we do not have the right attitude toward intercessory prayer—that is, prayer for others, both alive and dead. Both the Scriptures and the works of Christian writers give us ample and meaningful examples of intercessory prayers. The most beautiful of those come from Jesus himself, who interceded with God on behalf of his followers. Saint Augustine's *Confessions* also contain many prayers of this kind. Below is one such example, a prayer to God on behalf of his late mother, St. Monica:

"O God of my heart, my praise, my life, I will for a little while disregard her good deeds, for which I joyfully give you thanks, and pray to you now for my mother's sins. Hear me through that healing remedy who hung upon the tree, the medicine for our wounds who sits at your right hand and intercedes for us. I know that she dealt mercifully with others and from her heart forgave her debtors their debts; do you then forgive her any debts she contracted during all those years after she had passed through the saving waters. Forgive her, Lord, forgive, I beg you."[43]

Augustine's spiritual journey was long, complicated, and riddled with difficulties. With the passage of years he came to understand how much he owed to the intercessory prayers of his mother. That is why he wanted to repay her kindness.

Similar is the story of our own spiritual journeys. At first we say that God controls all, yet we act as if everything was completely determined by ourselves. We throw ourselves into different ventures, care about many things at once, and explore our options. We keep running as the spirit of our times dictates. At some point, however, we discover that all that workaholism neither bears the expected fruit nor provides the feeling of true happiness, so we start leaving more space for God. We begin to mature spiritually and pray more for others so that they may open their hearts to God's grace and let him transform their lives. This is how intercessory prayer, with which we entrust both the living and the dead to the merciful God, develops in our souls.

May we extend such prayers during Lent and ever more fervently pray to God, through St. Augustine and St. Monica, for our fellow men. Through prayer we too open ourselves up to the mercy of God.

---

[43] *Confessions* 9.13.35 (234).

32

"The proud looked on and fumed with anger"

—*Confessions* 8.2.4

❑ ❑ ❑

In the eighth book of his *Confessions* Augustine recalls meeting an elder priest by the name of Simplicianus, the spiritual father of St. Ambrose. After hearing about Augustine's experiences, his discovery of Christianity and journey toward it, Simplicianus tells a story of a well-known Roman orator and writer Victorinus, who bears similarities to Augustine. Victorinus converted to Christianity, and since he was a figure of fame and respect his baptism was received with joy by many of the city's inhabitants.

"He threw off the shamefacedness provoked by vanity and became modest in the face of truth: suddenly and without warning he said to Simplicianus, who told this tale, 'Let us go to church: I want to become a Christian.'

"Hardly able to contain his joy, Simplicianus went with him. He was initiated into the first stage of the catechumenate, and not long afterward he gave in his name, asking for rebirth in baptism. Rome stood amazed, while the Church was jubilant. The proud looked on and fumed with anger; they ground their teeth in impotent fury; but as for your servant, the Lord God was his hope and he had no eyes for vanities or lying follies."[44]

[44] *Confessions* 8.2.4 (188).

Today's gospel reading also talks about conversion and be-
lieving in Christ. Jesus encounters an unhappy man, blind since
birth. He performs another miracle and returns the man's sight.
When this man, now healed but rejected by the Pharisees, meets
Jesus for the second time he confesses his faith in the Messiah.
He is reborn spiritually, as well as physically.

The two conversions, one from the gospel and another from
Confessions, took place under different circumstances. In both
cases, however, people opened up to God's grace and changed
their thinking and conduct.

The further one wanders away from God, the more com-
plete the joy of finally accepting faith. That might be one of the
most mysterious principles of the human soul, which like many
spiritual phenomena often contradicts the principles of logic.
Perhaps because of that the reactions of some of the witnesses
were surprisingly similar: the Pharisees steadfastly stood by their
opinions—because "never since the world began has it been
heard that anyone opened the eyes of a person born blind" (John
9:32)—and those who witnessed the conversion of Victorinus
"fumed with anger [and] ground their teeth in impotent fury."
Both were oblivious to their own blindness, and they were content with the knowledge they already had and wanted no more.

That is the danger that threatens all of us as well: closing off,
defending opinions we already have, closing our eyes and ears
for what the Lord can reveal. How can Jesus heal someone from
blindness who is convinced that he sees everything just fine and
has no need for a doctor?

Protect us, Lord, from that kind of proud delusion and open
our minds and hearts to your offer of healing.

33

"Anyone who does truth comes to the light"

—*Confessions* 10.1.1

❏ ❏ ❏

Light and truth—two words that often recur in St. Augustine's *Confessions*. The fact is hardly surprising, considering the author's lengthy journey through darkness. Perhaps that is why since his conversion he so much appreciated walking in the light. The search for truth had been his lifelong quest, and conversion became the pivotal point. Yet the God that found Augustine was both close and distant to him, well-known and mysterious. That is why even years after his conversion, he still wrote passionately about his desire to know God better. Augustine asks God to open his soul to him and illustrates the beautiful relation between light and truth, for he who loves the truth walks toward the light.

"Let me know you, O you who know me; then shall I know even as I am known. You are the strength of my soul; make your way in and shape it to yourself, that it may be yours to have and to hold, free from stain or wrinkle. I speak because this is my hope, and whenever my joy springs from that hope it is joy well founded. As for the rest of this life's experiences, the more tears are shed over them the less are they worth weeping over, and the more truly worth lamenting the less do we bewail them while mired in them. You love the truth because anyone who does truth comes to the light. Truth it is what I want to do, in my heart by confession in your presence, and with my pen before many witnesses."[45]

Nicodemus also searched for truth and light. He represented a group of well-educated Jews who tried to open themselves to Jesus and his mission but did not sufficiently understand his teachings. Nor were they brave enough to publicly ask Jesus for answers to the questions bothering them. Nicodemus, who found it difficult to comprehend the need of rebirth as taught by Jesus, came to see Jesus at night and listened attentively to the teacher's explanations.

Jesus told him mostly about God's love toward humanity, "for God so loved the world that he gave his only Son, so that everyone who believes in him may not perish but may have eternal life" (John 3:16). He then revealed to Nicodemus that "the light has come into the world, and people loved darkness rather than light because their deeds were evil" (John 3:19).

Light and darkness, truth and falsehood, good and evil—these are the realities described in the Gospel of John and in St. Augustine's *Confessions*. They are not theoretical matters, for we know from personal experience that we are called each day to declare for one or the other. It might be comforting to know that these are the difficulties shared also by Nicodemus, Augustine, and numerous others from the pages of Scripture and two thousand years of Christian history. These choices manifest themselves before every believer and help our faith grow and lead us to the absolute Truth and Light.

Let us ask God, through the intercession of St. Augustine, to grant us perseverance in that journey, that we may see a ray of the Light that we believe to one day see in its full splendor.

[45] *Confessions* 10.1.1 (237).

34

"You yourself are ever the same"

—*Confessions* 8.3.6

□ □ □

There are numerous passages in the Holy Bible that describe the longing of humanity for God. It is enough to quote just a few fragments of the Psalms: "O God, you are my God, I seek you, my soul thirsts for you; my flesh faints for you, as in a dry and weary land where there is no water" (Ps 63:1); "My soul longs, indeed it faints for the courts of the Lord; my heart and my flesh sing for joy to the living God" (Ps 84:2).

One may also find passages of Scripture that show the longing of God for humans, as in the parable of the Prodigal Son read in churches today. "But while he was still far off, his father saw him and was filled with compassion; he ran and put his arms around him and kissed him" (Luke 15:20). The text makes no mention of "longing," but it is the father who sees his son first, and it is he who first gets emotional, runs toward his child, and embraces and kisses him. Augustine comments on the parable in the following way:

"The joy of your eucharistic assembly wrings tears from us when the story is read in your house of a younger son who *was dead, but has come back to life, was lost but is found.* You express your own joy through ours, and through the joy of your angels who are made holy by their holy charity; for you yourself are ever the same, and all transient things, things which cannot abide constantly in their mode of being, are known to your unchanging intelligence. What is going on in our minds, then, that we should be more highly delighted at finding cherished objects, or having them restored to us, than if we had always kept them safe?"[46]

During one of his General Audiences, St. John Paul II said: "Man, in whose footsteps follows God, can sense His presence, he bathes in light that follows him and hears a voice calling from afar. He then ventures out to search for God, who searches for him: the seeker begins to search; the loved begins to love. Today we try to describe this fascinating relation between the initiative of God and man's response and in it we find a fundamental component of religious experience."[47]

Just as the Prodigal Son left his father, so may we abandon God, try to live away from him, and search for happiness on our own. We will, however, quickly become disappointed, because we were created such that without God we may never be truly happy. God does not forget about us, just as the father in the parable never forgot his son and longed for his return.

It is good to reflect on those times in our own lives and spiritual history when we felt stronger than ever that God longs for us and awaits our return. Blessed are those times, for they show that in our relation with God he is always ahead, he is always first, and he searches for us before we search for him.

[46] *Confessions* 8.3.6-7 (189–90).
[47] Saint John Paul II, General Audience, July 5, 2000.

35

"I questioned my soul, demanding why it was sorrowful"

—*Confessions* 4.4.9

❑ ❑ ❑

Augustine writes of a close friendship he experienced as a young man in his hometown of Thagaste. He grew up with his friend, they shared interests, and studied and played together. From the pages of the *Confessions* we learn that Augustine's friend was never a fervent believer, and Augustine led him even further away from religion, which brought tears to the eyes of his mother. Augustine admits that when he was away from his friend he felt completely lost. One day the unforeseeable happened: Augustine's friend became gravely ill. When he ran a high fever and his condition was deemed serious, he was baptized. The youth soon felt better and when Augustine allowed himself to make light of the sacrament in the presence of his friend, he was reproached and forbidden to talk about it. A few days later when Augustine was absent, the condition of his friend worsened and he soon died.

"Black grief closed over my heart and wherever I looked I saw only death. My native land was a torment to me and my father's house unbelievable misery. Everything I had shared with my friend turned into hideous anguish without him. My eyes sought him everywhere, but he was missing; I hated all things because they held him not, and could no more say to me, 'Look, here he comes!' as they had been wont to do in his lifetime when he had been away. I had become a great enigma to myself, and I questioned my soul, demanding why it was sorrowful and why it so disquieted me, but it had no answer. If I bade it, 'Trust in God,' it rightly disobeyed me, for the man it had held so dear and lost was more real and more lovable than the fantasy in which it was bidden to trust. Weeping alone brought me solace, and took my friend's place as the only comfort of my soul."[48]

We can clearly see that the friendship between Augustine and the young man was very close. Their relationship was the kind that not only makes us see the friend in a different light but changes our views on others whom we meet, as well as our own lives. There can be no friendship with an abstract entity; there can be no friendship alone. Friendship is always between two people and is fulfilled in a meeting of both. It requires them to exchange experiences, and even the smallest of kind gestures that symbolize the gift of oneself made to a friend. Friendship changes us and helps us overcome our shortcomings and egoism, for true friendship is a demanding venture.

Years later, when Augustine wondered why he despaired so deeply after his friend's death, he came to the conclusion that their relationship lacked the presence of God. In reality "blessed is he who loves you, and loves his friend in you."[49] May these words help us to appropriately experience friendships, which are vital for our spiritual growth.

---

[48] *Confessions* 4.4.9 (97–98).
[49] Ibid., 4.9.14 (101).

36

"For this gift I offered you no sacrifice"

—*Confessions* 4.16.31

❑ ❑ ❑

When he was just under twenty years of age, Augustine took on the difficult task of reading one of Aristotle's most important works, the *Categories*. He had heard about it from his Carthaginian teachers of rhetoric, who spoke of it almost religiously. The young and talented Augustine read the book with interest and, to his surprise, understood it without too much difficulty. Furthermore, when he discussed the *Categories* afterwards with scholars, he quickly discovered that they could offer him little more than what he inferred from his own reading. Perhaps at the time he was not yet aware of the special talents that had been given to him. He later reflected on that experience in his *Confessions*:

"My swift intelligence and keen wits were your gift; you know it, O Lord my God. Yet for this gift I offered you no sacrifice. It therefore worked not to my advantage but rather to my harm, because I took care that this excellent part of my substance should be under my own control, and I did not guard my strength by approaching you, but left you and set out for a distant land to squander it there on the quest for meretricious gratifications. What profit was this good gift to me when I failed to use it well? It only made me less able to appreciate how very difficult these liberal arts were for even the most zealous and clever to understand. I found this out only when I tried to expound them to my pupils, among whom only the brightest could follow my explanation without dragging."[50]

How do we handle the talents that have been given to us and others to develop? On one hand, we all sometimes feel a slight sting of jealousy when we see others' accomplishments and the greatness of their skills and successes. We might not even be as jealous of the results as we are of the ease with which they were achieved. We have to pay for the miserable fruits of our labor with disproportionate amounts of sweat. We forget that from the spiritual standpoint daily effort is more important than an occasional victory.

But there is another danger in this, perhaps even graver than jealousy: the temptation to consider the talents ours by right, as if they were the products of our own will. Augustine gave in to this impulse and for many years regarded his extraordinary abilities as self-evident and took them for granted. Only when he started working as a teacher did he notice significant differences in the mental faculties of his pupils. Certain seemingly straightforward questions proved difficult even for the brightest of them. This provoked their teacher to contemplate the issue, but it took a long time for Augustine to see the grace of God Almighty in the talents with which he was blessed.

Father Tadeusz Król, Spiritual Director at Płock Seminary for many years, used to say when asked about the question of talents given by God and our attitudes toward them: "The beautiful things in life are all God's gifts . . . and we must constantly thank God for his gifts."

---

[50] *Confessions* 4.16.31 (111).

37

"They think themselves exalted to the stars and brilliant"

—Confessions 5.3.5

❏ ❏ ❏

Augustine did not find God through philosophical deliberations while under the influence of the Manichean sect. Their doctrine did not address the issues most important to Augustine; seeing no alternative, he remained a part of their group and kept telling himself that they might help him find happiness in the future. He eagerly awaited an encounter with a famous Manichean bishop in Carthage named Faustus, but upon meeting him he quickly realized the priest was chaotic in thought and poorly read. Bishop Faustus was unable to give answers to Augustine's questions, a failure that he humbly admitted.

Augustine was once again disappointed and, to a certain extent, ceased to be interested in Manichean teachings. Yet he continued with his philosophical quest. What he lacked was the humility in his approach to the religion so fervently practiced by his mother and the faith in God that rewards those who search with a humble heart.

"For great are you, Lord, and you look kindly on what is humble, but the lofty-minded you regard from afar. Only to those whose hearts are crushed do you draw close. You will not let yourself be found by the proud, nor even by those who in their inquisitive skill count stars or grains of sand, or measure the expanses of heaven, or trace the paths of planets. . . . They do not know [your only-begotten Son] as the Way whereby they can climb down from their lofty selves to him, and thus by him ascend to him. Of this Way they know nothing; they think themselves exalted to the stars and brilliant. But they have crashed down to earth and their foolish hearts are darkened."[51]

Augustine held the accomplishments of the scholars of his day in high regard, especially in the field of astronomy, where they were able to precisely predict the eclipses of the sun and the moon. But he was not afraid to harshly criticize some of them: "in their impious pride they draw away from you and lose your light, because these scholars who foresee a future eclipse of the sun long beforehand fail to see their own in the present."[52]

We can suppose that if Augustine were writing today he would admire the programmers, doctors, and engineers of our times. Yet he would urge them and us alike who benefit from their accomplishments to reflect on the progress of civilization with greater humility and, even more so, on the influence of technological advancement on our spirit. We need to present an attitude of the experienced and well-equipped mountaineer who is persistently conquering a jagged peak. The view is ever more stunning, but the climb ever more strenuous. Even the smallest movement is important. A wise mountaineer occasionally takes a deep breath and calmly looks up and down to check his bearings, the way ahead, and the changing weather.

Saint Augustine encourages us to take such a contemplative, calm and humble "breath" during Lent so that we may not presume ourselves as brilliant as the stars above.

---

[51] *Confessions* 5.3.3-5 (115–16).
[52] Ibid., 5.3.4 (116).

38

"Nothing should be regarded as true because it is eloquently stated"

—*Confessions* 5.6.10

❏ ❏ ❏

The culture in which St. Augustine grew up was focused on words, both spoken and written. Schools and universities taught rhetoric, considered one of the most important areas of education from antiquity until the Middle Ages. Augustine was a diligent student of rhetoric and had a firm grasp on it, which proved very useful first in the courts and then in the schools. He quickly realized that a skilled lawyer may achieve his goal and successfully defend the accused even if the latter is in fact guilty of the crime. In his film *Augustine: The Decline of the Roman Empire* director Christian Duguay shows how the son of St. Monica skillfully secured the release of a defendant who shortly afterward committed an even greater crime. Because of this and similar experiences, Augustine reflected in his *Confessions*:

"For some time, though, you had been teaching me in wondrous, hidden ways, my God (and I believe what you have taught me because it is true; there is no other teacher of truth except you, though teachers aplenty have made a name for themselves in many a place); so I had already learned under your tuition that nothing should be regarded as true because it is eloquently stated, nor false because the words sound clumsy. On the other hand, it is not true for being expressed in uncouth language either, nor false because couched in splendid words."[53]

Today's passage from the Gospel of John confirms the truth of St. Augustine's words. It contains a monologue of Jesus directed at the Jews. They too spent a lot of time analyzing words of the Old Testament prophesizing the coming of a Messiah. They awaited him fervently and described him in many ways, but they focused more on the form than the content. Jesus tells them: "You search the scriptures because you think that in them you have eternal life; and it is they that testify on my behalf. Yet you refuse to come to me to have life" (John 5:39-40).

These are the paradoxes in the conduct of the young and talented Augustine, as well as the older and more experienced Jews from the times of Christ. But it also concerns us. Bombarded every day by a constant flow of information from radio, television, newspapers, and the Internet, we may easily become lost and lured astray by sophisticated language—which not only aims at shocking audiences, drawing their attention, and inciting interest, but often hides spiritual voids, groundless accusations, promotion of improper conduct, and ridicule of the church and belief in God.

We must ask God, through the intercession of St. Augustine, for the gift of clarity in sifting through the constant flow of information, so that we may separate the useful from the chaff, that which helps us achieve salvation from that which leads us astray.

[53] *Confessions* 5.6.10 (120).

39

"To bring my steps back to the straight path"

—*Confessions* 5.8.14

□ □ □

In 383 A.D., the twenty-nine-year-old Augustine decided to leave Carthage and travel to Rome. Based on the information relayed in his *Confessions*, we can point to a few reasons that prompted the already famed rhetoric teacher to make such an important decision. First of all he considered the popular opinion that students in Rome were better behaved, more diligent, and more interested in the subjects of their studies than their Carthaginian counterparts. Second, the capital of the Roman Empire drew talented people with the prospects of higher pay and career opportunities. Augustine's mother, the pious Monica, did not share her son's conviction about his decision and to the very end hoped that he would yield to her pleas and remain in Carthage—or at least take her with him. Under the excuse of saying farewell to a friend at the harbor, Augustine secretly sailed away, leaving his mother praying at the nearby Chapel of St. Cyprian.

The bishop of Hippo describes those events in his *Confessions*, noticing above all God's mercy and the divine hand that directed his actions:

"It was you, *my hope and my inheritance in the country of the living*, who for my soul's salvation prompted me to change my country, and to this end you provided both the goads at Carthage that dislodged me from there and the allurements at Rome that attracted me; and this you did through the lovers of a life that is no more than death, who on the one hand behaved insanely and on the other held out to me vain promises. To bring my steps back to the straight path you secretly made use of both their perversity and mine."[54]

Our perception of certain events, especially painful experiences, changes significantly over time. We look differently not only at the times of sickness or misfortune, but also on the attitudes of our parents, teachers, and superiors toward us. At the time we might have been convinced that they were wrong, that we surely knew ourselves better, yet as the years go by we reassess past events and discover a new meaning previously hidden from our sight. Furthermore, we realize that we develop through certain conflicts and reconciliations, through darkness and light, through the goodness of some and the obstacles set by others. Ancient Romans used to say *per aspera ad astra*—through hardships to the stars.

Saint Augustine shows that we must reconcile with our past and notice the presence of God, who sometimes shows us the way through people representing unacceptable attitudes, who are sometimes outright unfriendly, and leads us through painful situations. God allows for those experiences to, in the words of Augustine, bring our steps back to the straight path, purify our hearts, help us grow in faith, and make our conduct more like that of his Son.

[54] *Confessions* 5.8.14 (123).

40

"With magnificent confidence he proclaimed the true faith"

—*Confessions* 8.2.5

☐ ☐ ☐

Among the persons described in the eighth book of *Confessions* was Victorinus, a rhetorician famous in Rome. It is no wonder that his conversion to Christianity caused great public interest. In the days preceding his profession of faith, the priests offered to let him make his statement privately, as was often done in the case of famous persons, but Victorinus chose to proclaim his salvation through faith publicly. He reasoned that just as he made speeches as a rhetorician openly, so he could not now shy away from publicly professing his Christian belief. Saint Augustine describes and comments on his previous attitudes:

"As he climbed up to repeat the Creed they all shouted his name to one another in a clamorous outburst of thanksgiving – everyone who knew him, that is; and was there anyone present who did not? Then in more subdued tones the word passed from joyful mouth to joyful mouth among them all: 'Victorinus, Victorinus!' Spontaneous was their shout of delight as they saw him, and spontaneous their attentive silence to hear him. With magnificent confidence he proclaimed the true faith, and all the people longed to clasp him tenderly to their hearts. And so they did, by loving him and rejoicing with him, for those affections were like clasping hands."[55]

Victorinus had seemingly done nothing out of the ordinary: he professed his faith in the same fashion as many other citizens of the declining Roman Empire had done. Yet it was he that earned special recognition and praise from St. Augustine, who at that moment deeply desired to follow in his footsteps.

People of all times need witnesses to faith. This has been the case ever since the time of Christ himself, as illustrated in today's gospel. When the guards told the priests and Pharisees, "Never has anyone spoken like this!" (John 7:46), they did not say anything extraordinary but honestly stated what they had seen and experienced. They became authentic witnesses for those who doubted or spoke against Jesus.

No exceptional feats are necessary to become a witness to faith in Christ but ordinary honesty, courage, and consistency. We often see how public figures in the world of politics or culture do not present an attitude toward faith that we might expect of them, in the name of misunderstood tolerance or due to opinions of others. It truly is a shame, since so many of them were once solidly grounded in Christianity and owe so much to the church.

But during Lent we must also look more closely at ourselves. How often do we give in to the pressure of our surroundings and let ourselves be convinced that religion is a private matter? We are often extremely reticent with religious gestures, wearing a cross, prayer, reading of the Scriptures in the presence of others, public admissions of faith, and so on. Do we not, in a way, deny Christ by this kind of conduct?

May today's reading of the gospel and the passage from the *Confessions* stimulate us to reflect on those matters and encourage us so that we would no longer be ashamed of our faith but rather become its unimpeachable and courageous witnesses.

---

[55] *Confessions* 8.2.5 (189).

41

"From this springs our grief if someone dies"

—*Confessions* 4.9.14

□ □ □

Augustine often wrote about friendship in his *Confessions*. He saw the special role it plays in human life and spiritual development. When we read his words it is hard not to get the impression that his views on the subject evolved as some of his own friendships grew stronger and others vanished, leaving behind sadness or disappointment. He became convinced that true friendship must include God. That way, even if a friend is lost due to unforeseeable circumstances, understandably causing pain, we may find solace in the knowledge that the God in whom we loved our friend can never be lost.

"Our conscience feels guilt if we fail to love someone who responds to us with love, or do not return the love of one who offers love to us, and this without seeking any bodily gratification from the other save signs of his goodwill. From this springs our grief if someone dies, from this come the darkness of sorrow and the heart drenched with tears because sweetness has turned to bitterness, so that as the dying lose their life, life becomes no better than death for those who live on. Blessed is he who loves you, and loves his friend in you and his enemy for your sake. He alone loses no one dear to him, to whom all are dear in the One who is never lost. And who is this but our God, the

God who made heaven and earth and fills them, because it was by filling them that he made them? No one loses you unless he tries to get rid of you."[56]

Today's gospel reading also talks about friendship: the friendship between Jesus and Lazarus. Saint John writes that when Jesus learned about the death of Lazarus, he wept, which did not often happen to our Savior. The Jews aptly noted: "See how he loved him!" (John 11:36).

When reading the above passage from *Confessions* and today's gospel we should take a look at our own friendships, both past and those that currently help us in spiritual growth—even if we have to overcome obstacles, make sacrifices, and face doubts to maintain them. Father Jan Twardowski writes: "Friendship is an immensely important thing, but not everyone finds it in their life. Unlike love, it is always reciprocated. One can be hopelessly in love for a lifetime, but one cannot be a friend alone."[57] Have we been blessed with experiencing such true friendship in our lives?

Friendships are essential because they help us open up to others, see them in different ways, enjoy life, and change our attitudes toward the people whose paths we cross every day. When we reflect on friendship after reading today's gospel and the words of St. Augustine, we must remember to include God in our everyday relationships. Without God true friendship is impossible, and there are only poor substitutes, obstructing instead of supporting our spiritual development.

[56] *Confessions* 4.9.14 (101).

[57] Jan Twardowski, *Autobiografia*, vol. 1 (Kraków: Wydawnictwo Literackie, 2006), p. 143.

42

"I see something not accessible to the scrutiny of the proud"

—*Confessions* 3.5.9

❑ ❑ ❑

Man longs for God because that is his nature. In the case of the young Augustine, this longing was strengthened by his pious mother Monica, who cared deeply about a Christian upbringing for her son. Even though Augustine had wandered the spiritual wilderness for many years, his yearning for Someone who could satisfy his desire for happiness did not go away but only grew stronger and burned deep inside him. He was impressed by the reading of Cicero's *Hortensius*, which encourages readers to search for wisdom without seeking any practical gains. Christ's name was nowhere to be found in *Hortensius*, so Augustine began to read the Scriptures. He approached them, though, just as he would any other work and failed to open his heart and mind to its principal Author. He was disappointed again.

"Through your mercy, Lord, my tender little heart had drunk in that name, the name of my Savior and your Son, with my mother's milk, and in my deepest heart I still held on to it. No writing from which that name was missing, even if learned, of literary elegance and truthful, could ever captivate me completely. Accordingly I turned my attention to the holy scriptures to find out what they were like. What I see in them today is something not accessible to the scrutiny of the proud nor exposed to the gaze of the immature, something lowly as one enters but lofty as one advances further, something veiled in mystery. At that time, though, I was in no state to enter, nor prepared to bow my head and accommodate myself to its ways."[58]

Longing for God is also the theme of today's gospel reading: "Now among those who went up to worship at the festival were some Greeks. They came to Philip, who was from Bethsaida in Galilee, and said to him, 'Sir, we wish to see Jesus'" (John 12:20-21).

The Greeks mentioned in the gospel attempted to overcome their difficulties by their own efforts, such as reading valued texts or taking opportunities to act and learn, just like Augustine did for many years. Of course God can change us within a very short timeframe, but more often than not it takes a long process of purification—one in which God is the dominant factor and whose work we can only help or hamper.

When we read today's passage from the gospel and the words of St. Augustine's *Confessions*, we should attempt to foster the longing for God's presence in our lives that has been planted in our hearts. It will never be fully satisfied during our earthly journeys, but it can bring us plenty of joy, enthusiasm, and hope.

[58] *Confessions* 3.4.8–5.9 (80).

43

"You know how much you have changed me"

—*Confessions* 10.36.58

❑ ❑ ❑

Saint Augustine's *Confessions* are a contemplation of God's goodness and mercy at work in the author's life. After his conversion, as he reflected on his past life, particularly the faults of youth, Augustine saw God's plan leading him. From the perspective of time, past events acquired a completely new meaning. Even the most simple of gestures, encounters, and words became signs of God searching for him. Most important, however, Augustine thanked God for forgiving the transgressions of his youth, which stemmed from the misunderstood concept of freedom.

Likewise, the woman mentioned in today's gospel reading did not properly understand and exercise the freedom given to her by God. Caught committing adultery, she was brought before Jesus by the Pharisees to be judged. But our Savior's response was different than what they expected. Christ not only refused to condemn her but he forgave her sins.

Augustine surely pondered this passage time and again. He wrote about the actions of God reaching out to man in the following way:

"Can there be for us any route back to hope other than your mercy, of which we have proof already because you have begun to change us? You know how much you have changed me, for you began by healing me of the itch to justify myself, so that you could be compassionate to all my other iniquities as well, heal all my ailments, rescue my life from decay, crown me in pity and mercy and overwhelmingly satisfy my desire with good things. You crushed my pride by inspiring in me reverential fear, and you made my neck submissive to your yoke. And now I wear it and find it benign."[59]

Strange indeed is our God, who does not condemn an adulteress, and blesses Augustine, who wandered aimlessly in spiritual wilderness, with intellectual prowess and spiritual graces. Thanks to God, he was able to turn back from his wicked path and start his life anew. And strange is our God who is partial to sinners, visits them where they dwell, and forgives their sins.

But it is exactly this kind of God who is our only hope. What would become of us if God presented himself only to the perfect, did not forgive our sins, and turned away from us because of our transgressions?

How comforting are the words of today's gospel reading and St. Augustine's *Confessions*, because they present an image of God whose mercy overcomes our sins and weaknesses. They can become our own "blessed faults" and start us off on a personal, spiritual journey.

Jesus directs his words to each and every one of us: "Neither do I condemn you. Go your way, and from now on do not sin again" (John 8:11). We can feel how those words set us free and how they fill our hearts with joy and strength. Because of them even inevitable suffering, hardships, fatigue, illnesses, and cares acquire a new meaning. To paraphrase the words of Augustine, we endure them and find them benign.

[59] *Confessions* 10.36.58 (275).

44

"Could you rebuff her plea for your aid?"

—*Confessions* 5.9.17

□ □ □

Augustine sailed from Carthage to Rome, leaving his mother behind. She prayed fervently and complained to God, believing that it was not only her son who left her but the Lord himself. The poor soul was not aware how much joy God had prepared for her in the form of her son's departure. Despite this difficult separation from her child, not only did she not stop praying but did so ever more passionately and entrusted her physically distant son to the merciful God.

Some of the most moving fragments of the *Confessions* are devoted to her prayer, perseverance, trust, and patience. Monica's style of prayer, her pleas to God, and her ways of dealing with painful experiences are worth a closer look.

"Would you, O God of all mercy, spurn the broken, humbled heart of a chaste and temperate widow who was untiring in her acts of charity, attentive to the needs of your saints and faithful in serving them? Never a day would pass but she was careful to make her offering at your altar. Twice a day, at morning and evening she was unfailingly present in your church, not for gossip or old wives' tales but so that she might hearken to your words, as you to her prayers. Could you, then, whose grace had made her what she was, disdain those tears and rebuff her plea for your aid, when what she tearfully begged from you was not gold or silver, not some insecure, ephemeral advantage, but the salvation of her son?"[60]

Penitence, humility, prudence, and attention to the voice of God—these are some of the characteristics of Monica's prayer in which she pleaded with God for the salvation of her son's soul. She was also known to give out alms and visited the church twice daily.

At the time of the *Confessions*, Augustine's mother had already been dead for more than a decade, yet she was still very much present in his mind and heart. As he progressed in the spiritual assessment of his life, he realized more and more how much he owed to her prayer. And yet he did not know everything about Monica and her faith—some things she told him herself, others he understood on his own, and more still were related by friends.

While reading St. Augustine's words on this day, how can we not think about our own mothers, both alive and those who are already with the Lord? As the years go by, we understand more and more how important it is to have a believing and loving mother, one willing to sacrifice everything for the good of her children. From our own experience and observations we know that mothers like that are not only a thing of the remote past. In these times, too, God gives to the world mothers of heroic faith, patient, penitent, and trusting prayer, and big, loving hearts.

On June 14, 1987, during his third pilgrimage to Poland, Saint John Paul II prayed at the grave of Fr. Jerzy Popiełuszko alongside his parents. "Mother, you have given us a great son," John Paul II said to Marianna Popiełuszko. "It was not I," she replied. "God gave him through me to the world."

---

[60] *Confessions* 5.9.17 (126).

45

"I hung keenly upon his words, but cared little for their content"

—*Confessions* 5.13.23

❑ ❑ ❑

Augustine's stay in Rome was indeed very short. The students in that city have proven to be no more diligent and honest than their Carthaginian counterparts. Augustine was quickly disappointed with teaching them and realized that such a place and position would not give him true happiness. Unexpectedly, he received an offer of assuming the prestigious post of rhetoric teacher in the imperial capital of Milan through Symmachus, the prefect of Rome. He accepted gladly and soon set out from Rome heading north. The pious Bishop Ambrose was diligently performing pastoral duties in the city of Milan and would later play an important role in Augustine's conversion. Toward the end of the fifth book of the *Confessions*, he describes his first impression of the famed priest and preacher:

"This man of God welcomed me with fatherly kindness and showed the charitable concern for my pilgrimage that befitted a bishop. I began to feel affection for him, not at first as a teacher of truth, for that I had given up hope of finding in your Church, but simply as a man who was kind to me. With professional interest I listened to him conducting disputes before the people, but my intention was not the right one: I was assessing his eloquence to see whether it matched his reputation. I wished to ascertain whether the readiness of speech with which rumor credited him was really there, or something more, or less. I hung keenly upon his words, but cared little for their content, and indeed despised it."[61]

When Augustine met Ambrose for the first time in his life, he was stricken above all by his human virtues: openness, kindness, and a good heart. The bishop of Milan must have had those in abundance, since Augustine was not afraid to state that he was welcomed like a son.

Ambrose did not immediately try to convert the young but already famous rhetoric teacher or touch upon subjects directly relating to faith and the church. For Augustine's idea of faith then was very different from the one he presented in his theological dissertations years later after his conversion. At the time he was convinced that faith is above all the result of one's own examinations, efforts, work, and philosophical inquiries. It took a lot of effort, wisdom, and patience on Ambrose's part to convince Augustine that faith is primarily a gift from God, who kindly regards those who open their hearts and minds. It is not man who is supposed to find the Truth, Ambrose said to him once, but simply allow the Truth to find him.

[61] *Confessions* 5.13.23 (131).

46

"I listened to him straightforwardly expounding the word of truth"

—*Confessions* 6.3.4

❑ ❑ ❑

Augustine's mother Monica surprised him with a visit in Milan. Her son informed her that he had left the ranks of the Manicheans and was still searching for truth and happiness. She intensified her prayers and listened to Ambrose's sermons with utmost piety while her son became more interested not only in the bishop's eloquent speech but also his personal lifestyle. He admired Ambrose's methodical style of work and devotion to the people. Augustine craved long and calm discussions with the bishop, but because of the large numbers of faithful waiting for their chance to meet the priest, he had to settle for brief, albeit very rewarding, encounters.

"At most, I could only put a point to him briefly, whereas my inner turmoil was at such a feverish pitch that I needed to find him completely at leisure if I were to pour it all out, and I never did so find him. Nonetheless I listened to him *straightforwardly expounding the word of truth* to the people every Sunday, and as I listened I became more and more convinced that it was possible to unravel all those cunning knots of calumny in which the sacred books had been entangled by tricksters who had deceived me and others."[62]

Augustine was lucky to have the pious Monica as his mother and the devout and enlightened Bishop Ambrose as his spiritual guide. It seems that in the matters of faith, he owed the most to those two persons. His mother was always with him in prayer, and Bishop Ambrose interpreted the most profound passages from the Holy Bible, expounded the truths of faith, and explained moral principles.

But is it that these kind of people were given by God only to Augustine and a handful of other chosen people? Lent is an opportunity to look back at our spiritual history and gratefully remember those who selflessly offered us help and kindness and shone light on our dark paths. Some among them surely were clergymen, our parish priests, vicars, catechists, confessors, and nuns. We must remember them, especially now, when the negative conduct of so many clergy is paraded in the media.

I believe that after some time of honest introspection, we can all recall our own Ambroses—surely less outstanding than the bishop of Milan, less proficient in explaining the Holy Bible, and less talented at preaching. But it is they whom God chose to put before us on our spiritual paths, despite their weaknesses.

We might reproach ourselves for not loving them enough, for being self-centered, and for not thanking them while we could still stand up and defend their names. But all that will become possible if we apply, even partially, what they taught and encouraged us to do in our lives.

[62] *Confessions*, 6.3.4 (138).

47

"I had been arguing blindly in the objections I raised against your Catholic Church"

—*Confessions* 6.4.5

❑ ❑ ❑

Augustine was fascinated with the person of Ambrose, although at the beginning he regarded him chiefly as a man of success. He was a skilled orator, loved by Catholics and respected even by those outside the church. He preached and taught with deep conviction, which revealed that he had attained a state of internal peace and happiness. Augustine, however, was not aware of the bishop's daily struggles and the fight he faced against the enemies of his community, both internal and external. As a matter of fact, Augustine himself had been one of the latter, and in his *Confessions* describes his attitude toward the church at the time:

"The anxiety which gnawed at my inner self to determine what I could hold onto as certain was the more intense in proportion to my shame at remembering how long I had been deluded and beguiled by assurances that falsehoods were certain, and had in my headstrong, childish error babbled about such very dubious things as though they were proven. Later on it became clearer to me that these tenets were false; but at the time I was at least certain of this, that while they were uncertain I had for a while held them to be certain, and had been arguing blindly in the objections I raised against your Catholic Church. I had not yet come to accept her teachings as true, but at least I now knew that she did not teach the doctrines to which I had gravely objected."[63]

In the *Confessions* Augustine shows how his opinion of the church evolved throughout the years—from the times of vigorous criticism until the day he became the head of a diocese. The above passage should encourage us to ask: How do we view the church and what is our stance toward the many attacks directed against the community of Christ?

Pope Benedict XVI appealed to the media for a more balanced and factual reporting on church matters. There is, in fact, a puzzling consistency in the negative interpretation of certain events, decisions, and trends. Of course weaknesses, sins, and failures are present in the church, for it is an institution in which human and divine elements intertwine. But one cannot overlook its goodness or purposefully ignore it. Nonbelievers often regard the church as just one of many social and religious organizations, and that is their right. However, without faith it is impossible to fully comprehend Christian theology, spirituality, the concept of life, and so on. Augustine understood this only after his baptism, and only then did he have the courage to admit his past errors and unjustified hostility.

Those of us believers who write and speak of the church should remember the words of St. Thérèse of Lisieux from a time when the church was especially subject to severe criticism: *J'aime l'Église ma Mère.* "I love the Church my Mother."

I believe that Augustine would be delighted to repeat those words. The knowledge that we are not only members of the church but also participate in creating it and, above all, love it, makes us consider and weigh our own sins and those of our brothers and sisters in a different way.

---

[63] *Confessions* 6.4.5 (139).

48

"He said nothing which offended me"

—Confessions 6.4.6

❑ ❑ ❑

Augustine was becoming more fascinated with Ambrose's teachings, especially with his interpretations of biblical texts. He clearly remembered the disappointment after his first reading of the Scriptures. He had approached them as a teacher approaches a textbook, without the humility required of someone in search of happiness through contemplation of the word of God. While listening to Ambrose's explanations, he was surprised how clearly those same words spoke to his heart and enlightened his mind.

"Another thing that brought me joy was that the ancient writings of the law and the prophets were now being offered to me under quite a different aspect from that under which they had seemed to me absurd when I believed that your holy people held such crude opinions; for the fact was that they did not. I delighted to hear Ambrose often asserting in his sermons to the people, as a principle on which he must insist emphatically, *The letter is death-dealing, but the spirit gives life*. This he would tell them as he drew aside the veil of mystery and opened to them the spiritual meaning of passages which, taken literally, would seem to mislead. He said nothing which offended me."[64]

---

[64] *Confessions* 6.4.6 (140).

"The letter is death-dealing, but the spirit gives life" (2 Cor 3:6). These words of St. Paul from his second letter to the Corinthians must have been spoken by Ambrose often, since Augustine claims that they became a principle of his teaching. The bishop pointed to some scholars of the Scriptures and how they were unable to open their hearts and minds to the meaning that had been hidden behind those words.

In today's passage from the gospel, Jesus identifies that same fault in the Jews who did not discover the message of the Old Testament, but focused solely on the literal word and consequently rejected the Messiah sent to them. "The Jews took up stones again to stone him. Jesus replied, 'I have shown you many good works from the Father. For which of these are you going to stone me?'" (John 10:31-32).

Scholars in Jesus' day spent a lot of time reading and contemplating the Scriptures. They tried unreasonably hard to understand and explain single words and expressions and show their specific and literal meaning while neglecting the hidden implications significant to spiritual life.

Augustine explains: "In plain words and very humble modes of speech it offered itself to everyone, yet stretched the understanding of those who were *not shallow-minded*. It welcomed all comers to its hospitable embrace, yet through narrow openings attracted a few to you."[65]

Let us try to open our minds and hearts to the words God will direct at us during this coming Holy Week, so that we may too get close to Him through the "narrow openings."

[65] Ibid., 6.5.8 (142).

49

"How tardily do we return to you!"

—*Confessions* 8.3.8

❑ ❑ ❑

Through referring once more to the conversion of the famous rhetorician and writer Victorinus, Augustine tries, at least partially, to understand the nature of the return of sinful man to the merciful God. He stresses that God never leaves his creation, but shines a beacon of light for those who have wandered away. At the same time, the author is aware that any human reasoning on the subject can only lead to partial discovery, since God remains the Great Unknown. That is why his philosophical exploration grows into a pious prayer and a plea to God.

"Ah, how high you are in the heights of heaven, how deep in the depths! From no place are you absent, yet how tardily do we return to you! Come, Lord, arouse us and call us back, kindle us and seize us, prove to us how sweet you are in your burning tenderness; let us love you and run to you. Are there not many who return to you from a deeper, blinder pit than did Victorinus, many who draw near to you and are illumined as they welcome the light, and in welcoming it receive from you the power to become children of God?"[66]

---

[66] *Confessions* 8.3.8–4.9 (191).

Today's gospel reading also touches upon the subject of the search and return to God. The miraculous resurrection of Lazarus caused various reactions among the Jews: some believed in the Savior while others, especially the rulers, were afraid that Jesus might speak out against the Romans and put the whole nation in danger. Following the advice of the high priest Caiaphas, they decided to sacrifice one life for the good of many. Others who had come to Jerusalem for Passover were, according to St. John's account, "asking one another as they stood in the temple, 'What do you think? Surely he will not come to the festival, will he?'" (John 11:56).

Lent is a special time of searching for God. We try to find God as hard as our limited abilities and strength will allow, but if we rely solely on them we may be sorely disappointed. For in reality we require a stirring of the heart that comes only from God and not from within. Saint Augustine tried to achieve happiness through his remarkable talents alone, yet he became ever more miserable. The high priests and Pharisees from today's gospel were so sure of themselves that they did not even attempt to view the Messiah among their people in a different light. The choices and attitudes of humans vary greatly; indeed, so do their reactions to God's initiatives.

Let us open ourselves up to the Light, the only Light, that will allow us to climb up from the depths of illusory self-sufficiency and develop a different outlook on our lives. Then may we notice that the change is easier than we had thought and that God was closer than we had imagined, and we shall be given a special capacity to become God's children.

50

"The light of certainty flooded my heart"

—*Confessions* 8.12.29

◻ ◻ ◻

On Palm Sunday, when we remember Jesus' joyful arrival at Jerusalem, we abandon the chronology of the events in Augustine's life for a bit and look at a fragment of *Confessions* that describes the moment when the author could finally say after a long search and many dilemmas, questions, and doubts: "I believe." He describes this crucial event in much detail, as he must have recalled it many times in his contemplations. It might be surprising to learn how many tears St. Augustine shed, how he looked for solitude and was unsure of what was happening to him—although deep down he understood that he was experiencing something profound.

"I flung myself down somehow under a fig-tree and gave free rein to the tears that burst from my eyes like rivers, as an acceptable sacrifice to you. Many things I had to say to you, and the gist of them, though not the precise words, was: 'O Lord, how long? How long? Will you be angry for ever? Do not remember our age-old sins.' . . . I went on talking like this and weeping in the intense bitterness of my broken heart. Suddenly I heard a voice from a house nearby—perhaps a voice of some boy or girl, I do not know—singing over and over again, 'Pick it up and read, pick it up and read.' . . . I snatched [the book] up, opened it and read in silence the passage on which my eyes first lighted:

. . . Put on the Lord Jesus Christ, and make no provision for the flesh or the gratification of your desires. I had no wish to read further, nor was there need. No sooner had I reached the end of the verse than the light of certainty flooded my heart and all dark shades of doubt fled away."[67]

Can we remember the moment when we consciously told God, "I believe"? When was it? In what situation? Did we also shed tears? Did we look for solitude? Or perhaps our confession of belief took place in a completely different setting?

We should ask these and similar questions on this Palm Sunday when we read and contemplate the account of Christ's passion and listen to the last words our Savior spoke during his earthly journey. They should be a constant source of reflection and inspiration for us. Words once spoken by the mysterious person to St. Augustine, "Pick it up and read, pick it up and read," relate to all of us and are an encouragement to ponder the life and death of Christ even today. It will give us the strength we need in our daily lives. It will give us the courage that we often lack in today's world, so often hostile as it is to the spirit of the Gospel—courage to profess our faith in him who preached the word of grace.

After years of philosophical explorations, St. Augustine came to the conclusion that the Christian God is completely different than how he had imagined, and by reading the account of the Passion he understood that it is enough to simply not oppose God in our daily lives and open up to God's initiative. This attitude he recommends to all of us: follow the path marked out for us by Jesus himself. Only through it can we arrive at his kingdom: "I am the way, and the truth, and the life" (John 14:6). No, from this day on there can indeed be no more doubt about it.

---

[67] *Confessions* 8.12.28-29 (206–7).

51

"How you loved us, O good Father"

—*Confessions* 10.43.68

❑ ❑ ❑

Every year on Palm Sunday we listen to the account of Christ's
passion. Depending on the current condition of our life, we
tend to discover different details of this immensely rich story.
Sometimes we may not realize why a certain passage of the
Passion appeals to us more than another. We can suppose that
St. Augustine also contemplated the apostolic account of the
torment, death, and resurrection of our Lord Jesus.

The bishop of Hippo stressed that our Savior's gift of redemption has changed the condition of the whole of humanity, each
and every one of us. In his commentary he points primarily to
the infinite love of God the Father who sent his Son to us so
that humanity could be elevated to the ranks of children of God
through his suffering and not in any other way.

"How you loved us, O good Father, who spared not even your
only Son, but gave him up for us evildoers! How you loved us,
for whose sake we who deemed it no robbery to be your equal
was made subservient, even to the point of dying on the cross!
Alone of all he was free among the dead, for he had power to
lay down his life and power to retrieve it. For our sake he stood
to you as both victor and victim, and victor because victim; for
us he stood to you as a priest and sacrifice, and priest because

sacrifice, making us sons and daughters to you instead of servants by being born of you to serve us. With good reason is there solid hope for me in him, because you will heal all my infirmities through him who sits at your right hand and intercedes for us."[68]

God, who gave up his only Son to be crucified, loves us in a special way. We might sometimes wonder why God chose such a path for our salvation, a question that often renders us speechless. The magnificent work of Jesus Christ still strongly influences even our everyday lives, as in the case of Augustine, a great sinner turned great saint.

The Lord wants to heal all of our infirmities. May this knowledge stay with us when we attentively listen to the account of Jesus' capture, rejection by his own people, ridicule, crucifixion, and mockery from the feet of the cross. Mark the Evangelist describes in his relation of the events how, at the moment of Jesus' death, "the curtain of the temple was torn in two, from top to bottom. Now when the centurion, who stood facing him, saw that in this way he breathed his last, he said, 'Truly this man was God's Son!'" (Mark 15:38-39). A centurion, a pagan with no deeper understanding of the Jewish faith and messianic prophecies, professed faith deeply and spontaneously.

Let us hold the centurion's *Credo* as our own as we start another Holy Week of our lives. And may we give thanks to God for the infinite love he has for us through his crucified and resurrected Son Jesus Christ. "How you loved us, O good Father!"

[68] *Confessions* 10.43.68 (282).

52

"Your only Son . . . has redeemed me with his blood"

—*Confessions* 10.43.70

☐ ☐ ☐

As the years of our lives go by, we interpret and experience Christ's passion in different ways. In our youth we may have been more drawn to its descriptive form and how it was read in our churches. In adulthood we try to read into individual sentences and find a higher meaning relevant to the current state of our lives.

While writing his *Confessions*, St. Augustine performed an in-depth analysis of his life and past actions primarily through the lens of God's mercy, embodied in a special way in the redemptive work of Jesus Christ. In the passage below he describes how he could not come to terms with his own sinful past, but sought to live in solitude to repent and pray for the graces he lacked. Yet he overestimated the value of his efforts; only the inspired words of Christ, who died for all, helped him develop a new look on his past and present.

"Filled with terror by my sins and my load of misery I had been turning over in my mind a plan to flee into solitude, but you forbade me, and reminded me, *that they who are alive may live not for themselves, but for him who died for them.* See, then

Lord: I cast my care upon you that I may live, and I will contemplate the wonders you have revealed. You know how stupid and weak I am: teach me and heal me. Your only Son, in whom are hidden all treasures of wisdom and knowledge, has redeemed me with his blood. Let not the proud disparage me, for I am mindful of my ransom."[69]

We can look at our past in different ways. In his account of Christ's death, St. Luke notes that two criminals were crucified alongside Jesus. Both were guilty of numerous crimes and sinned throughout their lives, but at the moment of their crucifixion they behaved in completely different ways. One spewed abuse at Jesus, while the other pleaded: "Jesus, remember me when you come into your kingdom" (Luke 23:42). The Savior promised him that he would stand in paradise with him that very day.

We do not know whether the good criminal had the opportunity to meticulously reflect upon his life before that moment, but he was given a unique opportunity and he took it without a second thought.

Two completely different stories—that of the good criminal and that of St. Augustine—illustrate how God gives everyone some kind of an opportunity in life. He grants it in different settings and moments of our journeys. Jesus redeemed all with his blood and opened the gates of heaven for us.

We cannot forget our weaknesses, but today, as we reflect on Christ's passion, may we first and foremost remember the price Christ paid for us and its unimaginable redemptive power.

---

[69] *Confessions* 10.43.70 (283).

53

"What agonizing birth-pangs tore my heart"

—*Confessions* 7.7.11

❑ ❑ ❑

As he listened to sermons and teachings of St. Ambrose in the thirty-first year of his life, Augustine became more and more fascinated by the Christian God, but he still could not comprehend the origin and purpose of evil and suffering. He writes about it in the seventh book of his *Confessions*, in which he mentions Jesus Christ more often than in the previous six. (Up to this point he chiefly addressed God the Father). It seems that this shift was caused by his reading of the letters of St. Paul. Perhaps the story of Paul's life and conversion made Augustine contemplate those words more often than other works: the letters touch upon the redemptive work of the Son of God, belief in whom is a gift that opens up to grace, reaches true freedom, and seeks answers to the questions of evil and suffering in the brilliance of the life and work of Christ.

"I believed . . . that in your Son, Christ our Lord, and in the holy scriptures which the authority of your Catholic Church guarantees, you have laid down the way for human beings to reach that eternal life which awaits us after death. These beliefs were unaffected, and persisted strong and unshaken in me as I feverishly searched for the origin of evil. What agonizing birth-pangs tore my heart, what groans it uttered, O my God!

And there, unknown to me, were your hearkening ears, for as I labored hard in my silent search the mute sufferings of my mind reached your mercy as loud cries."[70]

Augustine's suffering was primarily spiritual. He could never reach true happiness, so he kept longing and asking questions that caused pain and, in his words, made his heart groan.

Different indeed are the paths that lead to God. The Apostle Paul was blessed with a radical conversion while on the way to Damascus, the faith of St. Augustine was born in long pangs of agonizing pain, and different still was the faith of Mary of Bethany, portrayed in today's gospel reading. First she listened attentively to Christ's teachings, later she witnessed the miraculous resurrection of her brother Lazarus, and in today's passage—as if intuitively sensing future events and the death of Jesus—she poured perfume on his feet and wiped it with her hair. All the while she does not utter a single word; at this stage of love they are truly unnecessary.

Mary of Bethany, Paul of Tarsus, and Augustine of Hippo all found the answer to questions about evil and suffering in human life thanks to believing in him who suffered greatly, bearing the cross and staggering toward Calvary toward death and resurrection.

Through those great saints, O Lord, help us to cry loudly to your mercy and, especially during this Holy Week, open our hearts and minds to your salutary teachings and grace.

[70] *Confessions* 7.7.11 (168).

54

"My swollen pride subsided"

—*Confessions* 7.8.12

❑ ❑ ❑

Augustine was getting closer to believing in Christ, yet a tempest raged in his soul that he could not put into words even for those closest to him. He found it difficult to describe what had been going on in his heart and mind even to himself. Later, when he recalled those past experiences, he was convinced that God alone had known and heard all and that his internal anxiety had been spiritually meaningful. But he did not see it at the time; Augustine still wanted to get close to God on his own. Yet he was aware of his weaknesses and the need to cleanse his heart of his pride, which made it impossible for him to have an objective view of his spiritual condition.

"My swollen pride got in the way and kept me from you, and my face was so puffy that my eyes were closed. But you, Lord, abide for ever and will not forever be angry with us, for you have taken pity on us who are earth and ashes; and so it was pleasing in your sight to give new form to my deformity. You goaded me within to make me chafe impatiently until you should grow clear to my spiritual sight. At the unseen touch of your medicine my swelling subsided, while under the stinging eye-salve of curative

107

pain the fretful, darkened vision of my spirit began to improve day by day."[71]

Today's gospel reading also talks about pride but in a different context. Jesus parts with his disciples saying: "Little children, I am with you only a little longer. You will look for me; and as I said to the Jews so now I say to you, 'Where I am going, you cannot come'" (John 13:33). "Peter said to him, 'Lord, why can I not follow you now? I will lay down my life for you.' Jesus answered, 'Will you lay down your life for me? Very truly, I tell you, before the cock crows, you will have denied me three times'" (John 13:37-38). Peter's reaction was spontaneous and honest, and without a second thought he reassured Jesus that he was willing to lay down his life for him. He did not know that through those words he showed overconfidence in his own strength to help Jesus. How wrong was he, as in reality he was a fearful man and it was rather he who needed support from Jesus.

Peter, Augustine, and many other saints had to go through the purifying fire of God's love to experience the unseen touch of God's medicine. In today's gospel Jesus shows us the power without which we cannot follow him to Golgotha. This power is Jesus himself.

Help us, Jesus, to experience the mystery of your holy Passion, so that we may abandon our pride, confidence in self-reliance, and need to search for happiness on our own. May we open up completely to your redemptive work and the grace that you offer.

---

[71] *Confessions* 7.7.11–8.12 (169).

55

"I disregarded the idols of the Egyptians"

—*Confessions* 7.9.15

□ □ □

In his *Confessions*, Augustine describes how God opposes the haughty and blesses the humble. One particularly proud acquaintance of Augustine gave him some works of the Neoplatonists. The man's intention was completely different, yet as Augustine kept reading them, he began to wonder why Neoplatonists often mentioned the eternal Word, but failed to mention its workings since its moment of incarnation. He quickly realized that through Neoplatonic works alone he would not learn much about what most fascinated him: the earthly life of Christ, his torment, death, and resurrection. Therefore he read the New Testament and clearly noticed how the entirety of the Holy Bible demonstrates one magnificent creation of the same God, but also reveals human infidelities. It is enough to mention the golden calf cast by the Israelites during Moses' absence or the betrayal of Judas from today's gospel reading.

"I set my heart upon the gold which at your bidding your people had brought out of Egypt, because wherever it was, it belonged to you. So you told the Athenians through your apostle that in you we live and move and have our being, and that indeed some of their own authorities had said this, and unquestionably those books I read came from there. I disregarded the idols of the Egyptians, to which they paid homage with gold that belonged to you, for they perverted the truth of God into a lie, worshipping a creature and serving it rather than the creator. Warned by these writings that I must return to myself, I entered under your guidance the innermost places of my being; but only because you had become my helper was I able to do so."[72]

The Israelites, gifted by God with freedom, betrayed Him and turned to golden idols. In today's gospel we read about how Judas betrayed his master for money, despite being chosen and beloved by him. Jesus said: "'Woe to that one by whom the Son of Man is betrayed! It would have been better for that one not to have been born.' Judas, who betrayed him, said, 'Surely not I, Rabbi?' He replied, 'You have said so'" (Matt 26:24-25).

The golden calf in the desert, Judas' betrayal on the night of Holy Thursday, Neoplatonic rejection of the redemptive work of Word incarnate—these are the different forms of humanity denying God. Fortunately they are not the last words spoken in the great battle between good and evil; that is spoken by God alone. And it is important for us when we struggle with doubts, fears, difficulties and when we go from great love to fierce hate and from deep faith to denial.

Help us in our daily lives, Lord, to turn away from the various false idols offered by the modern world, and strengthen the conviction and faith in our hearts and minds that only you can give us true happiness and eternal life.

[72] *Confessions* 7.9.15–10.16 (171–72).

56

"The record of debt that stood against us was annulled"

—*Confessions* 7.21.27

❏ ❏ ❏

Toward the end of the seventh book of the *Confessions*, Augustine recalls how voraciously he read books inspired by the Holy Spirit. Everything that had at first seemed convoluted and at times self-contradictory now appeared amazingly simple and soothing for his restless soul. He saw how contemplation of the Holy Bible lead him straight to its principal Author, who releases the broken reader from death and gives him true happiness. Christ liberates man from the sentence that was passed on him at the very beginning of his existence.

"What is a human wretch to do? Who will free him from this death-laden body, if not your grace, given through Jesus Christ our Lord, whom you have begotten coeternal with yourself and created at the beginning of all your works? In him the ruler of this world found nothing that deserved death, yet slew him all the same; and so the record of debt that stood against us was annulled. None of this is to be found in those other books. Not in those pages are traced the lineaments of such loving-kindness, or the tears of confession, or the sacrifice of an anguished spirit offered to you from a contrite and humbled heart, or the salvation of a people, or a city chosen to be your bride or the pledge of the Holy Spirit, or the cup of our ransom. Not there is anyone heart to sing, *Shall not my soul surrender itself to God? For my salvation comes from him. He is my very God, my Savior.*[73]

The words of St. Augustine acquire a truly special meaning on Holy Thursday, when we listen intently to the reading of the Gospel of John about Jesus, who "got up from the table, took off his outer robe, and tied a towel around himself. Then he poured water into a basin and began to wash the disciples' feet and to wipe them with the towel that was tied around him" (John 13:4-5). Here is our Master who proceeds to wash his disciples' feet in the manner of a servant. He does it calmly, gracefully, and with dignity. There is no rush, every gesture carries meaning, and the atmosphere in the room is truly special. That is indeed *not* the God from the Neoplatonic works read by Augustine.

Yet just as Augustine could not understand the Scriptures for years, this gesture of God might be surprising and hard to comprehend for us as well. We can only hope to one day understand more. Let us accept Jesus' service with trust and gratitude. Sometimes we may think that everything must be understood and explained, but our God, fortunately, does not have to abide by the rules of human logic.

On this Holy Thursday let us look at the world—and especially our lives and God's goodness towards us—in a different way, so that we may see the great work done by Jesus two thousand years ago, when he annulled the record of debt that stood against us.

[73] *Confessions* 7.21.27 (182).

57

"Walk steadily in the way that leads there"

—Confessions 7.21.27

◻ ◻ ◻

"Come to me, all you that are weary" (Matt 11:28). With these words Augustine ends the seventh of thirteen books of his *Confessions*, while adding his own comment to the words of Christ in an attempt to convey (at least to a certain extent) the special atmosphere of a day like Good Friday. Augustine realized that God opened a new and unknown road in front of him, one that leads to the thing he so desired: true happiness. He also understood that one does not need philosophical preparation and the ability to conduct complicated theoretical deductions, for the Christian God is completely different than what he had previously thought.

"He is gentle and humble of heart, and you have hidden these things from the sagacious and shrewd, and revealed them to little ones. It is one thing to survey our peaceful homeland from a wooded height but fail to find the way there, and make vain attempts to travel through impassable terrain, while fugitive deserters marshaled by the lion and the dragon obstruct and lurk in the ambush; and quite another to walk steadily in the way that leads there, along the well-built road opened up by the heavenly emperor."[74]

God, who is gentle and humble of heart; God who hides great truths from the sagacious and shrewd and reveals them to little ones; God who points the way to the land of *differently* defined happiness—these are the new elements in Augustine's idea of God. He is now aware of the mistakes he has made in life. He vividly depicts a peaceful homeland that he had seen but could not find a way into it, so he wandered the wastelands among threats and ambushes.

He can see the way now, so he knows where to go and who awaits him. On this Good Friday, after several dozen of these short deliberations, we leave Augustine, who now crosses the threshold of faith. On this day the church reminds us of the unique path walked by Christ two thousand years ago, as he traversed Jerusalem's Via Dolorosa bearing his heavy cross. Martyrs and believers, wives and virgins, priests and laypeople, those known from the pages of church's histories and those unnamed, known only to God—all of them, throughout the ages, followed in his footsteps. They walked the road leading to the kingdom of God of which Jesus spoke and St. Augustine wrote. On this special day of the Paschal Triduum, let us pray to God in the words of Augustine:

"Give us peace, Lord God, for you have given us all else; give us the peace that is repose, the peace of Sabbath, and the peace that knows no evening. This whole order of exceedingly good things, intensely beautiful as it is, will pass away when it has served its purpose: these things too will have their morning and their evening. But the seventh day has no evening and sinks toward no sunset, for you sanctified it that it might abide for ever."[75]

---

[74] *Confessions* 7.21.27 (182–83).
[75] Ibid., 13.35.50–36.51 (379).